ENERGY MANAGER'S WORKBOOK

ENERGY MANAGER'S WORKBOOK

Based on the papers presented to the
Energy Managers' Workshops
organised jointly by the British Institute of Management
and the Department of Energy

Energy Publications (Cambridge)

First published in Britain in 1982 by Energy Publications (Cambridge)

© The British Institute of Management

ISBN 0 905332 22 9

Energy Publications (Cambridge) is the energy book publishing imprint of
Cambridge Information and Research Services Limited
Sussex House, Hobson Street, Cambridge, England

Printed in Great Britain by
St Edmundsbury Press, Suffolk

FOREWORD

by David Mellor MP

Parliamentary Under Secretary of State for Energy

The energy management movement has made a valuable contribution to the important objective of increasing the energy efficiency of industry, commerce, and local government in Britain. To support energy managers, the Department of Energy, as one of its initiatives in the training field, started in 1978 to run the National Energy Managers' Courses, with the full support of the fuel industries, and I was delighted when in 1981 the British Institute of Management joined us in running the courses, now known as Energy Managers' Workshops. These training courses have played a central role in training energy managers, especially those newly appointed, to plan and supervise the most cost-effective use of energy in their own organisation.

This book brings together for the first time the material written by the speakers at the workshops, without whom the workshops would not be possible. I congratulate the British Institute of Management on running the workshops, demonstrating their recognition of the importance of energy management as an integral part of each organisation's overall efficiency. I also welcome their initiative in making this most interesting and useful compilation available to a wider audience. Every energy manager, new or experienced, will learn something from reading the distilled wisdom of the energy conservation experts who have contributed to this book.

FOREWORD

by Roy Close

Director General, The British Institute of Management

BIM was very pleased to respond to the Department of Energy's invitation to join them in running the Energy Managers' Workshop—not only because this would make a valuable contribution to the national effort but because resource management in its wider sense is the natural concern of the Institute.

Energy management is unusual in that it is management without risk. Any well conceived investment of time or of money will produce a return and indeed one that is inflation proofed. As the cost of fuel increases so savings from conservation measures become greater. The only question on any investment is how great a return and over what period of time? Because of this, energy is particularly susceptible to the management process.

The workshop, and this book derived from it, sets out in practical terms how to go about energy management. After reading it and attending the course the energy manager will know how to go about his task. He will know which information to collect and how to use it. He will be able to set out his objectives so that he will know what it is he wants to achieve and the progress he is making. When he has difficulties he will know that his local Regional Energy Conservation Officer can put him in touch with an Energy Managers' Group, the members of whom will frequently be able to help. He should expect savings of between 10-30 per cent and more.

It is therefore with pleasure that I commend this book to energy managers as a sure guide to an important task.

Roy Close

CONTENTS

INTRODUCTION

The Energy Managers' Workshops posed an exciting challenge to BIM. They provided in one activity the opportunity for a two fold demonstration. Firstly, of the management process itself. Secondly, of the benefits to an organisation of the intelligent use of resources.

Energy management represents a perfect microcosm of the management process. We start with the misuse of people and resources. We end with their proper utilisation. The process of achieving this desired end encompasses the classical management activities—finding and classifying the facts, identifying areas for improvement, setting achievable targets, monitoring and controlling them, and motivating staff, all, to be effective, requiring technical knowledge.

Our own targets in setting up these workshops were clear. We wanted to equip delegates to go back to their organisations as competent energy managers. They should be capable of achieving measurable savings of between 10 and 30 per cent over the course of a year.

Our methodology was two-fold. It was to take delegates through the management process, and to make them competent by providing them with enough technical information, or the wherewithal to find that information. Our approach was to base the programme on the energy management needs of the conference centre itself, Ashorne Hill College, and to give delegates the opportunity to do on the workshop what they would do as energy managers on their return to work. We chose to be as practical as possible, and as far from the Ivory Tower as could be.

We started by describing the role of the energy manager with his need to influence and work through others. Terry Henshaw of Amey Roadstone took this session, and subsequently Bernard Lubert of Marks and Spencers, Peter Ibbotson of Sainsbury and Reg Harrison of British Home Stores. We then went on to a full day audit of the conference centre (Chapter 9). Setting that up was a major activity in itself. David Yuill spent nearly a week of his time on it, collecting energy bills, arranging metering, measuring up and generally preparing a comprehensive survey. The delegates thus had a very high standard to emulate and I believe they all found the exercise stimulating and demanding.

A day later, we visited the boiler houses and dirtied our hands with measuring instruments that Charles Hardy provided. On subsequent days with the help of HEVAC we talked about the principles of controls, looked at their costs and benefits, and examined control equipment. Barry Healey introduced us to the financial case, and we carried out a project evaluation on some of the recommendations of the Central Survey Report. We considered lighting with the Lighting Industry Federation, insulation with EURISOL, building services with Ken Spiers of Laing R & D and transport with Bill Kirkland of South Yorkshire PTE. We had a unique opportunity to cross examine representatives of the four fuel supply industries, and finished with a description of the current help available.

We were extremely lucky. We had the enthusiastic co-operation of the Department of Energy, the fuel supply industries and all the speakers and trade associations who participated. They really did help in an unstinting manner. It would be invidious to single out individuals as being particularly helpful, and I will reluctantly resist that temptation. But they all contributed to a worthwhile workshop, and I have listed all their names in Appendix I.

Note must also be made of the co-operation received from the staff of Ashorne Hill College and in particular their willingness for the premises to be used for the Energy Survey and for the results to be included in this Workbook.

In editing this Workbook, the publishers had one particularly difficult problem. They had to balance the need for technical information with the need to make the book readable for energy managers who were numerate but not themselves technical. To do this, they had to sacrifice a good deal of the technical information supplied to them. I believe they have achieved the right balance, and perhaps they might want to publish a technical textbook on energy conservation at a later date although the best way of getting all the technical detail is, of course, to attend one of the workshops.

Apart from this, our publishers had to face all the problems which are endemic to the publishing trade, but they have brought the book out successfully, and we are grateful to them for their effort.

Finally, a word about Gerry Coghlan, our Workshop Director. As an experienced engineer and past director of a major engineering group, he was an ideal man to chair the sessions. He had that little extra, a great sense of humour, that made the workshops go with a swing.

Peter Martin
Management Development Adviser
British Institute of Management

NOTES ON CONTRIBUTORS

Charles Hardy is an independent consultant specialising in the area of industrial boiler and burner combustion in which he is a recognised authority. He worked for many years for Hamworthy Engineering becoming the Chief Engineer of the Combustion Division. Mr Hardy is a consultant to a number of organisations including an international oil company for which he travels extensively. A Fellow of the Institute of Energy Mr Hardy is a regular lecturer and writer on combustion matters.

J Barry Healey is a Fellow of the Institute of Chartered Secretaries and a Member of the Institute of Management Consultants. After several years in banking he moved into industry eventually becoming Company Secretary and Financial Controller of an engineering group. Mr Healey spent six years with a major management consultancy and for the last five years has been in private consultancy practice.

Terry Henshaw is Group Electrical and Energy Engineer of the Amey Roadstone Corporation. He is the Chairman of the Avon and Somerset Energy Managers Group and a very successful and respected Chairman of the National Energy Managers Advisory Committee (NEMAC). Founded in 1981 NEMAC represents the energy managers groups, of which there are over 70 in the country, which in turn represents the interests of over 5,000 energy managers. Mr Henshaw is a member of the Advisory Council for Energy Conservation ex officio.

Bill Kirkland is the Controller of Engineering and Property Services with the South Yorkshire Passenger Transport Executive (SYPTE). Responsibilities cover all engineering related to vehicles, property, plant, equipment, etc. He is a Member of the SYPTE Management Board. Previous positions include Chief Engineer with Greater Glasgow PTE and the Greater Manchester PTE. Mr Kirkland is a Chartered Engineer and Member of the Institution of Mechanical Engineers.

Victor Neal spent six years in lighting research laboratories primarily concerned with light sources and photometry following an apprenticeship in the electrical industry. He has held a number of positions in Philips Lighting during the last 25 years ranging from Lamp Applications Engineer to Manager of the Project Engineering Department and is currently Manager of the Energy Advisory Group. Mr Neal is a Member of the Chartered Institution of Building Services.

Fred Ranson has been directly involved in industrial energy management for the last 10 years including positions with BL Cars (Component Division) and the East Anglian RHA. He has worked for the last two years for Johnson Control Systems and is now the company's Product Manager, Energy Systems. He is a Fellow of the Institution of Engineering Designers, a Member of the Institution of Plant Engineers and a Member of the British Institute of Management. Mr Ranson represents the Institution of Engineering Designers on the Watt Committee for Energy.

Michael Wells is a Senior Projects Engineer with Thorn EMI Limited. He has over 20 years experience in the lighting industry primarily concerned with all aspects of commercial and industrial lighting. His special interests are integrated design and energy management. Mr Wells is a past West Midlands Chairman of the Illuminating Engineering Society, a forerunner of the Chartered Institution of Building Services. As well as being a Member of the CIBS Mr Wells is also a Member of the Institution of Public Lighting Engineers.

Alan Williams led the successful energy management team in Pilkington Brothers plc from 1974 until 1981. Since then he has been a director of insulation contracting companies in the Pilkington group and is currently Marketing Director of Kitson's Insulation Contractors Limited. Mr Williams is a qualified physicist and carried out research into coal dust explosion for the then Ministry of Power before joining Pilkington Brothers in 1966 as a Fuel Technologist. He travelled extensively for the company on combustion and float glass problems before establishing a pollution control activity in 1971.

David Yuill is an independent energy consultant to industry specialising in energy survey work aimed at improving energy management capabilities. He qualified as a Fuel Technologist at Imperial College, London and has spent many years in manufacturing industry. He lectures regularly on energy management and was a consultant to the Department of Energy for an energy management film. Mr Yuill is a Chartered Engineer and Member of the Institute of Energy.

ILLUSTRATIONS

1

THE ROLE OF THE ENERGY MANAGER

Terry Henshaw

The transformation in energy costs over the past decade has led to the establishment of the energy manager as an essential part of the management team. For no organisation can expect to maintain its competitive position in the marketplace if it fails to ensure, with reasonable certainty, that its future supply of energy is secure and that there is strict control on how it is being used.

But the term 'energy manager' is relatively new and continues to be regarded with suspicion in some quarters. Perhaps not surprisingly when in a world where commercial interests are of paramount importance, technical innovation which calls for radical changes in established practices and the existing patterns of investment are usually unwelcome.

This chapter sets the scene for those that follow by defining the objectives the energy manager must pursue and the qualities he should possess if he is to prove successful. It also attempts to clear away at the outset some misconceptions, still too widely held, on the scope for improving energy efficiency in industry and commerce and the role the energy manager should play.

Attitudes to Energy Conservation

One of the prime functional tasks the energy manager faces is to change existing attitudes towards energy use particularly within the working environment. Conservation, and energy management generally, continues to be wrongly regarded by far too many as a short term expedient. It is still being said that once the good housekeeping and other basic techniques have been put into effect, then the present limit has been reached. It is then up to technology to provide for the future.

Those people could never be more wrong! Energy management is a long-term function which must shape, monitor, implement and control the way in which any organisation uses or plans to use that most vital and essential resource—energy.

Moreover a good deal of the suspicion encountered by energy managers stems from the somewhat indefinite nature of the job. But this is correct as energy management is a challenging multi-disciplinary task which contains as its base a large part of the other established functions which operate within industry and commerce.

This is not to say that its purpose is to compete with or encroach upon those established disciplines. The main objective is to provide a supplementary and additional function in a new and most necessary dimension.

In a broad sense, management may be defined as the direction, control and organisation of business, money, equipment and people towards a profitable goal. Energy managers must play a necessary part in the achievement of that objective. The correct approach to energy, and its use, is vital in ensuring the future profitability and competitive status of industry and commerce, which now faces a formidable obstacle—the availability and cost of all aspects of energy. The energy manager, therefore, fulfils a vital role within the wealth creating management team.

Necessary Qualities of the Energy Manager

The term manager implies the involvement of people and as it is people who use energy the energy manager is no exception. Certainly the need for the energy manager to manage people cannot be overstated.

The successful energy manager can therefore emerge from almost any background. Most seem to have one of the engineering disciplines as their foundation but this is not essential. A number of accountants, for example, have proved first-class energy managers.

Seven qualities come most readily to mind which the energy manager will need to develop. Firstly, he must be a good communicator having the ability to listen as well as talk. He should possess or develop the ability to use simple language and analogies as illustrations to ensure effective communication with all levels of people from director to machine operator. He must be a good administrator able to correlate factual data and information on energy matters, usage and equipment. Without such information there is no framework within which to manage, take decisions and justify expenditure. He must also be able to prepare clear, lucid, interesting and concise reports.

The energy manager will need to be broad minded and prepared to consider and examine all possibilities regardless of how unlikely they appear to be. He must be enthusiastic, articulate, persuasive and sure of his facts. He must be prepared to accept that his advice and knowledge, however right, will be ignored on occasions in some areas or parts of the decision making process. This may not be an indication of failure and it is important to establish the reason so that the method of approach can be changed in the future.

Finally, and above all, he must have a good understanding of people. The attitudes of individuals towards energy and its methods of use are vastly different. Many are reluctant to change without good cause their established practices or habits. In addition, they are unlikely to welcome being informed that they are using energy inefficiently. The approach must therefore be suitably diplomatic, and the energy manager must be thick-skinned in order to withstand the occasional and inevitable reaction.

The Objectives of Energy Management

Having described some of the more desirable qualities of an energy manager, it is important to be able to outline and explain the individual objectives which may well form the basic terms of reference of an energy manager.

These are listed in Table 1.1 and discussed below.

Information and Data

These areas are basically covered in the first objective of developing and maintaining an energy accounting system. The system will cover information on energy purchases, stocks and the monitoring of consumption.

To be effective each type of energy used in each area or production location should be separately monitored and recorded. To achieve this the energy manager must have free access to all data, invoices and financial statements relating in any way to energy purchases and consumption.

He will need to initiate the procurement and installation of suitable monitoring equipment and be responsible for the collation of the resulting data. The object is to show the true cost and consumption of energy at each point of use or section of the process etc. The true cost of the various types of energy used in each area or section must be accurately established if the cost effectiveness of each area of the plant or section of the process is to be assessed, and if future planning and action is to be reliable.

All energy data used to complete the audit system must be collected and recorded on a uniform basis, using a consistent common unit. Avoid the use at all costs of terms like gigajoules and the like. People just do not understand them and anyway all energy units are inter-convertible if necessary. Conversion to a standard kilowatt (kW) base has the advantage of everyone having a mental picture of its value or capacity.

Wherever possible energy consumption should be related directly to the activity, expressed as energy consumed per unit of output. This is important in setting economic and attainable targets.

TABLE 1.1: KEY OBJECTIVES FOR THE ENERGY MANAGER

1. Develop and maintain an energy accounting or audit system.

2. Co-ordinate the efforts of all energy users in the organisation helping them from a source of sound information to set tough but realistic targets.

3. Provide sound technical and specialist advice to all departments within the organisation on energy-saving equipment and techniques to promote the efficient use of energy.

4. Liaise with committees and working groups within the industry/sector and maintain contact with appropriate research organisations, professional bodies and government organisations to monitor, assess and apply all significant developments in the field of energy conservation.

5. Appraise and advise upon government funding and other schemes applicable to the organisation.

6. Examine, appraise and advise upon any political, legislative and regulatory measures relating to energy and assess the possible impact on the organisation's products and activities.

7. Remain up-to-date on the changing world and national developments on energy matters and advise senior management of the possible effects on the organisation.

For example, if the organisation produces washing machines, then so many units of energy will be required to produce that item. How can this be reduced? Is it necessary? Is energy being wasted? Can the design or product specification be changed to reduce the energy content? What quantities of energy do the support functions absorb in order to sustain the main production effort? Will the proposals be practical and cost effective?

The regular collection and collation of the right kind of data will quickly and accurately answer such questions as these, which are really concerned with accountability: knowing how much energy is used; how much it costs; where it is being used and who is using it wisely.

The energy manager will be the focal point for records of energy use and the person directly responsible for their analysis. He must also demonstrate that any data collected or provided by other people is not wasted. The results should be published and the potential areas for further detailed investigation highlighted. A simple graph rather than a table of figures is the best means of communication in this area. Graphs can also be used to provide a simple review of the progress to date.

It is vital to remember that all efforts must be cost effective and that any proposals for capital or indeed any expenditure must meet the existing investment criteria of the organisation. Companies are not in business to save energy at any price and any effort to persuade people to follow this course will only result in the destruction of credibility and future effectiveness.

Co-ordination and Support: The Energy Action Group

As it is most unlikely that the energy manager will have the direct responsibility for the implementation of these objectives (Numbers 2 and 3 in Table 1.1), they must be achieved from the co-operation and co-ordination of other senior responsible people in the organisation. Ideally these would be the respective heads of departments, as it is they who are accountable, responsible for, and have the authority to apply or discard the measures proposed by the energy manager within their respective areas.

As in any organisation, all sections or departments are designed to form an integral part of the total structure, so again everyone is involved. It may therefore be necessary to have a group of such responsible people meeting under the title of that unfortunate and often misappropriated word, committee. It is therefore better to use the term 'action group'. This avoids the use or creation of a committee as most people avoid or are suspicious of such gatherings. Where energy is concerned it is action that is required not lip service, therefore start as you mean to carry on and use the term 'energy action group'. A possible successful structure used by one company is shown in diagrammatic form in Figure 1.2. Whatever final structure is chosen the energy manager must be an integral part of it—always at the crossroads of interchange of information, co-ordinating and providing impetus to the action.

The final arrangement of the action group may adopt many forms, depending upon the purpose and structure of individual concerns. The principle must be adopted and applied to suit individual circumstances.

Since it is always easier to increase than reduce the number of people forming the group, begin with as few people as possible. The numbers can easily be increased at a later date if required. It may also prove to be simpler to co-opt people to discuss or examine specific subjects or potential areas of energy cost savings. But, as all action proposals emanating from the group must be cost effective, do not forget to include a senior 'financial' member of the team who can help to prepare or advise upon proposals for capital and revenue expenditure etc.

Select the members of the group from consideration of their particular skills, responsibilities and levels of authority, as it will be directly through these people that you will have that essential and direct communication with the general workforce. Group members drawn from different skills and areas will complement the energy manager and each other as effective energy management involves a part of all disciplines. In each case they will already be aware of the prospective pitfalls and other obstacles to proposals. They can also indicate possible short cuts or methods to increase the effectiveness of activities. Success depends upon the co-operation and application of the group members, therefore never undermine their respective functions.

The energy manager should not attempt to chair the group. The task will be better accomplished by a senior person such as a director. His presence will establish that necessary degree of authority and purpose to the group. The energy manager's main task will be to fulfil the two objectives and monitor and report on the progress of the measures 'actioned' and put into effect by the group. In a very large concern it may prove beneficial to have more than one action group covering different locations or activities. Again the energy manager must correlate and cross fertilise new ideas between each group.

Providing Technical Data

Access to technical information can be achieved in several ways, one of which is to create a technical library. As mentioned earlier, energy management is multi-disciplinary; it is also the basis of a whole new branch of technology which is producing equipment, ideas and systems designed to increase energy efficiency. The energy manager must be constantly aware of new techniques, of what equipment is currently available and of any other developments in this field.

The library will therefore consist of a file of product data, literature and application information describing these many products. The specialised equipment manufacturers and energy supply organisations all have specialists with wide experience of their product or service. These are an important source of experience and knowledge which can be complementary. Energy conservation techniques and experiences are now developing on a broad front. The energy manager will need to ensure that his knowledge develops at the same rate. As he will be responsible for the final application it is especially important that he learns to distinguish quickly between good, bad and indifferent systems and techniques. This gathering, application and processing of information can lead to the fulfilment of other essential objectives of an energy manager.

Liaison with External Sources

The energy manager will probably need to obtain the approval of his organisation before becoming fully involved with outside groups. It will be necessary to establish what aspects of the operation

FIGURE 1.2: THE ENERGY ACTION GROUP

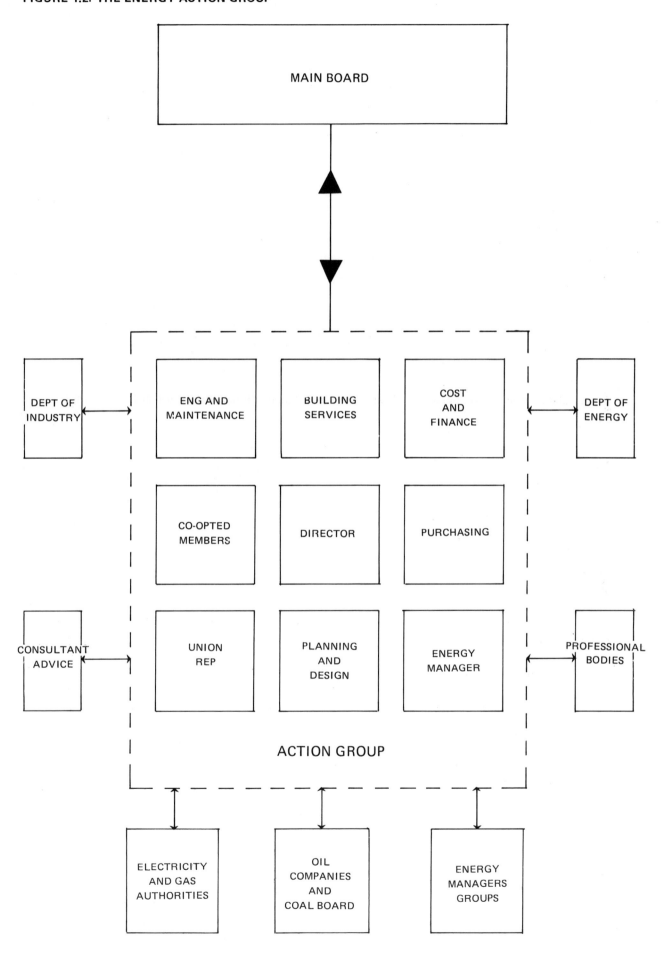

can be safely discussed for example when participating in industrial trade associations. All such groups operate through the exchange of ideas and experiences and the formulation of plans for the benefit of the industry as a whole. Such contact is to be considered a very necessary part of the energy manager's job as defined under Objective 4 in Table 1.1.

Publications must be obtained and read: conferences and suitable courses attended. One extremely valuable source of information and opportunity to learn from the experience of others is to join the local Energy Managers Group.

These are actively supported and encouraged by the Department of Energy and provide a direct link with government, research associations and information on support measures. The local Regional Energy Conservation Officer at the Department of Industry's regional office will advise. (See Appendix II). He will also provide booklets and information describing a wide range of measures including grants introduced by the government to promote the conservation of energy.

The contacts developed and information obtained through these channels will help fulfil the next two objectives: namely advising on government funds (Objective 5) and assessing any legislative changes (Objective 6).

Assessing the Future

Industry cannot operate profitably or efficiently without access to a secure and adequate supply of energy. The type of energy required will depend on the activity and it may well prove to be a mixture of oil, gas, electricity and, possibly, coal.

Unless attempts are made to read the energy future the effects of a shortage, a sudden price escalation and the cost of converting at short notice from one fuel to another could have a disastrous effect on profitability. It is essential to determine from the mass of data available the best possible future course of action.

Conservation and the efficient use of energy will figure centrally within this plan. The recent past, with the ten fold increase in oil product prices in as many years, needs little further comment, industrial fuel costs having risen twice as fast as the wholesale price index for all materials excluding fuel.

In the short term some slackening in this rate of increase is to be expected but there are few who predict major reductions in fuel prices. High energy costs seem set to stay for many years to come whilst in the longer term all forms of energy, and particularly oil, seem set to occupy an even larger share of operating costs than at present.

Energy is now an important factor in the decision making process and will in future have a marked effect on the viability of plans for investment in new products. No one but the energy manager is close enough to the energy scene to be able to interpret the overall picture as it slowly unfolds from year to year.

Where energy is concerned, it is not the capital cost of the plant which matters, it is the running or operating cost. Large investment involving depreciation or payback periods of over five to ten years can rapidly become uneconomic to operate due to the rising cost of energy. In addition to reading the future, the energy manager should be involved in all new projects involving any expenditure whatsoever. Remember that at present day prices the cost of an electric motor equals its running costs for around six months.

Reporting

The present and ever increasing importance of energy management ideally demands that the energy manager reports directly to the board or at least to a senior executive within the overall management structure.

As energy costs and usage involve every department or section of the organisation, then in order to be effective the status and set reporting procedure of the energy manager needs to be clearly defined.

Policy

Success or failure will depend upon obtaining the commitment of top management, the union and the total work force. Employees can quickly tell when an energy saving effort is just tokenism. The main giveaway is recognised as a lack of interest or support from the top. If efforts are to succeed, then management support requires much more than someone giving the nod to a conservation programme and assuming that each individual will just 'fit this little job' into his already busy schedule. If the commitment is not there, everyone including the energy manager could well be wasting each other's time.

One of the first jobs must be to draw up a comprehensive proposal suggesting the pattern of involvement of everyone from the main board to the shop or office floor. The proposals must outline the financial benefits which are likely to accrue in the short and longer term. From these will emerge the objectives which the board will be asked to endorse as a matter of firm company policy. This is the main licence for the energy manager to proceed. Once approved, the policy and its objectives must be widely circulated so that everyone knows of its existence and purpose.

Top management support must go beyond the usual letters of intent and general platitudes. It also means making the manpower and money available to do the job.

Health and Safety

An effective energy management programme will improve the profitability of the company together with job security and pay prospects. Whatever the course of action chosen it must always take into account any potential effect upon health and safety and pollution requirements.

To succeed, energy management must focus on the systematic measurement and control of energy which in turn gives improvements in working conditions with overall benefits to health and safety.

Codes of Practice

These are simply handbooks or basic manuals of good energy practices. They contain practical easily followed rules or advice relating to the methods of using energy within the organisation. Ideally, it is part of the role of the energy manager to prepare these in conjunction with the action group. Above all they must be practical and easily understood by everyone within the organisation.

They will be produced in simple booklet form and contain specific information on everything from switching off unnecessary lights to the efficient control of boiler plant and heat treatment processes. They may be prepared as a simple check list or in a comprehensive manual, dependent upon the complexity of the organisation. In each case they should be based upon simple logic and above all common sense.

Motivation and Training

The most significant problem in achieving changes in the individual attitude towards energy is the need to change long standing, deep seated customs and practice. In attempting to change these attitudes it must be the aim to make energy conservation an integral part of the routine practice of the organisation by making everyone aware of the need to conserve. It is a vital part of our future way of life. As was recently said 'you've got to be turned on if you're going to turn off'.

So, another part of the energy manager's activities must be public relations and training, making people aware of what is happening, why it is happening and what they can do to help. If the organisation has an internal newspaper or a P.R. department use it to the full. Seek the advice of the P.R. staff—after all communications and promotion are their business. Many concerns effectively use slogans, cartoon characters, posters, stickers and in-house competitions. Some even have a regular awards scheme. All promote the community spirit towards a common goal and even if there is only one winner of an award, others have tried, and each competitor makes an individual contribution towards the overall objective.

But beware, a P.R. approach although necessary can be short lived and difficult to sustain. The ultimate target must be to remove the control of energy from many to a relatively small number of people. This is achieved by automatic control systems, which of course can adopt many forms covering many different applications. Automated systems can also waste energy— if they are incorrectly adjusted or programmed then they are permanently wrong.

It is rightly said that money motivates. However, beware of any incentive scheme which incorporates payments for energy savings. The rising cost of energy, in spite of a vigorous conservation programme, can lead to a situation where no cash savings are realised even though energy is being saved. That situation will more than likely result in unhealthy mistrust and the possible collapse of the effort.

In-house training seminars are very productive providing they are properly organised and planned. In arranging these you should endeavour to use films and visual aids as much as possible. The advantage of seminars is that people are addressed as individuals. Therefore, keep the numbers down, and do not attempt to educate the whole work force at one session.

The seminars would also serve as training sessions where two way discussion is essential. These will identify problems and obstacles and in turn help overcome them. Involve all who attend. Everyone wants to learn but few want to be told. As a result all will benefit and areas can be identified where more specialised training would be even more beneficial, particularly if the presentation is pitched to a particular audience level. But never underestimate the audience, be patient and keep a sense of humour.

Priorities and Strategy

The best way for the newly appointed energy manager to establish himself is to concentrate on those areas likely to give the largest financial savings. The secondary, smaller savings can follow later. Ironic though it may seem one of the best weapons in the armoury will be an increase in the price of energy. The larger the increase the more aware everyone becomes of its value. The energy manager must be ready to take advantage of these situations immediately they arise.

The energy manager's main role is not to save energy himself but to organise, stimulate and encourage others. Success can be measured when the atmosphere has been created in which all have become energy managers.

Energy management is a long-term function of ever increasing importance. Perhaps the only certainty in this fast changing area is that those who take it up will find it a challenging and most rewarding task.

2
CARRYING OUT THE ENERGY SURVEY

David Yuill

Undertaking an energy survey is the vital first step for the energy manager as he embarks on his programme for improving fuel use efficiency and trimming energy costs. It will provide him with the basic data on current fuel practices within his plant and premises; data essential if his energy programme is to gain credibility and the eventual approval of senior management.

The objective of the survey is simple: to compare the amounts of the different fuels purchased over a period of time, say the last twelve months, with the process and heating energy requirements as established from an examination of the plant and a realistic assessment of the amounts of heat and energy which should be needed.

Accounting in this way for how and where fuel is used is vital. It will establish in the first instance how much of the fuel purchased simply goes to waste: a figure, often found to be between 20 and 40 per cent of the total and certainly of a size to interest senior and financial management if presented in the right way. It will also enable a sound approach to be taken to selecting the most suitable areas for early attention. It will rank these by potential savings and cost and provide the basic data for the financial appraisal, as detailed in Chapter 3. But above all it will show the organisation's energy consumption in total and in its constituent parts enabling the energy manager to develop an overview of his responsibilities and also to question whether existing practices remain appropriate to today's high cost fuel environment.

Help is to hand in this exercise through the Department of Energy's one-day Energy Survey Scheme. This enables organisations to reclaim currently up to £75.00 from the fee charged by a consultant for carrying out the survey from the Department as long as the report and application are made in the approved manner and the consultant is officially recognised.

But much can be done by the energy manager working on his own and even if a consultant is engaged he will require certain basic data which may need collecting over a lengthy period of time. The purpose of this chapter is to establish what information this is likely to be and to show how it can be collected. The chapter then goes on to describe a particular case study of an energy survey in an industrial plant. Attention is also drawn to the last chapter in the book which offers scope for putting into practice the techniques described in this chapter. It sets out the range of information on fuel consumption found to be to hand at a college used for the Energy Managers' Workshop. It lists the areas suggested for examination by the delegates, who subsequently undertook their own survey, and concludes with the text of the report presented to management. It follows the general pattern required in the Energy Survey Scheme by the Department of Energy and hence is illustrative of the type of report the energy manager can expect to receive on his own premises if he makes use of the scheme.

Principles and Practice

Finding out current consumption levels of fuel and power in the plant is the starting point for the energy survey. These can be ascertained most easily from an historical analysis of purchase invoices supplemented, as and when possible, by more frequent reading of total site, and if possible departmental, meters. Tests on individual plant and processes may also be undertaken.

Once this basic information is to hand it is possible to account for the use of fuel by comparing it with reasonable estimates of what the consumption should be, based on theoretical calculations and sometimes rule of thumb estimates. The whole, in terms of the total amounts of bought-in energy, must be compared with the sum of the parts, as evidenced from the individual plant and departmental investigations. Only in this way can possible inefficiencies be checked or identified in terms, for example, of distribution losses or wasteful plant loading.

The causes of the discrepancies, which will inevitably emerge, between actual and predicted energy consumption must then be investigated. This will reveal the extent of potential savings available, the cost and time needed to achieve them and an indication of the relative cost effectiveness of the alternative courses of action whether the investment costs be low, medium or high.

It is also important when undertaking the survey to look critically at individual processes or loads. Are there more efficient ways of achieving the required result? Perhaps the specification can be changed to reduce energy requirements? The survey should be used to question all the ways that energy is used in the organisation. Practices established years before, most probably in times of low fuel costs, may well no longer be justifiable.

At this stage sufficient data will be amassed to allow the financial appraisal to take place, as outlined in Chapter 3. Not only will this appraisal highlight what action is worthwhile in terms of the company's own financial standards, but it will also rank the various schemes to identify which should be tackled first.

The principle of accounting for known energy consumption can be applied in all main areas of fuel use and cost. Practical aspects will inevitably be encountered which vary from plant-to-plant and from process-to-process but certain procedures will emerge as common to all surveys albeit with their own modifications. Surveying in the three areas of process heating, space heating and electricity consumption and charges are now discussed separately.

Process Heating

Process heating energy requirements can usually be estimated from some form of heat balance. The performance of process plant, e.g. furnaces or dryers, can be measured in terms of their energy consumption in relation to output with the results indicating what proportion of fuel is being usefully applied and, possibly, where the rest is going. This type of exercise will focus attention on several key questions. Can plant efficiency be improved? Should the waste heat, having been reduced to the practical minimum, be recovered? Is there a use for such recovered waste heat? And, most importantly, can process specifications be changed so that energy requirements are reduced?

Measuring and improving the efficiency of boiler plant is a subject dealt with separately in Chapter 6. But at this stage it will be important to establish how much of the total steam, or hot water, is generated for the various process applications and how much is required to meet space heating needs.

Ideally the energy manager will have at his disposal strategically placed meters to provide this information. In practice he may be forced to adopt his own methods. For example when only one meter indicates the energy requirements of several consuming loads it may be possible to assess individual consumptions by noting the total usage for several different combinations of these loads. An example of this type of analysis is given in the case study at the end of this chapter.

Improvised metering of energy consumption is an important skill in energy management. What it may lack in detailed accuracy will likely be more than compensated for by its low cost and quick results permitting a speedy assessment of energy saving potentials. Other examples of useful substitutes for conventional fluid flow metering are weighing condensate to measure steam consumption and the use of elapsed time meters on oil and gas burners.

Space Heating

Approximate space heating requirements can be assessed using rough rules of thumb based on experience from buildings of similar construction and use. Examples of such 'guestimates' in particular conditions are the use of one gigajoule (equivalent to 277 kWh or 9.5 therms) per square metre a year, or 70 kilojoules per cubic metre an hour when the outside temperature is -1° Centigrade. If the plant's space heating requirements differ substantially from a reasonably assumed standard then further investigation is required. A more rational way of calculating heat losses is by using the following formula:

$$Q = \sum UA\,(t_{ei} - t_{eo}) + 0.33NV\,(t_{ai} - t_{ao})\ watts$$
Total Loss = Fabric Loss + Ventilation Loss

The fabric loss is calculated as the sum of the U values (heat loss characteristics—see page 69) of all the external areas involved (A) multiplied by the difference between the inside environmental temperature (t_{ei}) and the outside temperature (t_{eo}).

The ventilation loss is calculated as one-third of the number of air changes per hour (N) in the total volume of air in cubic metres (V) multiplied by the difference between the inside air temperature (t_{ai}) and the outside air temperature (t_{ao}).

The formula also indicates the relative importance of insulation and ventilation losses in any particular set of conditions. In larger buildings with high rates of air change, for example, it may well be that the size of ventilation loss is such that this should be tackled first before improving the insulation.

Environmental temperature (t_e) is a better index of warmth and comfort condition than the dry bulb air temperature (t_a). (This point is developed further on page 49). t_e is influenced partly by t_a but more so by the mean radiant temperature (t_r) which is the mean of the surface temperatures within the building or defined area. The relationship is two:one, radiant to air temperature in determining the environmental temperature.

Thus $\quad t_{ei} = \dfrac{1}{3}\,t_{ai} + \dfrac{2}{3}\,t_{ri}$

An understanding of this principle shows why radiant heating is more economical than warm air heating in certain conditions, and notably in buildings with high rates of air change. In one particular poorly insulated building, for example, the choice between radiant and warm air heating shows a markedly lower air temperature requirement with radiant heaters—see Table 2.1. This in turn will lead to lower ventilation loss and therefore to reduced total building heat loss.

TABLE 2.1: WARM AIR AND RADIANT HEATING REQUIREMENTS IN A POORLY INSULATED BUILDING

(°C)	Required Inside Environmental Temperature (t_{ei})	Inside Mean Radiant Temperature (t_{ri})	Inside Air Temperature (t_{ai})
Warm Air	16	13.8	20.5
Radiant Air	16	17.8	13.9

The table shows that to achieve an environmental temperature of 16°C (suitable for light factory work) the air temperature must be raised to 20.5°C if a warm air system is used whereas it can be as low as 13.9°C with a radiant system.

These particular figures do, however, relate to a specific example of a poorly insulated building. Conditions vary across industrial buildings for a variety of reasons and expert guidance should be sought in determining the suitability of alternative systems in individual circumstances.

Another factor to look out for in the space heating survey is the correlation (if any) between the load pattern and outside temperatures. After all in a well controlled system, other factors being constant, the space heat requirement of a building should be determined by the difference between inside and outside temperatures $(t_i - t_o)$.

Use should be made in this exercise of degree day data, now published monthly in the
Department of Energy's Energy Management newspaper. These figures, presented on a monthly
basis for 17 regions of the United Kingdom, represent the daily difference in °C between a base
temperature of 15.5°C (60°F) and the 24-hour mean outside temperature when it falls below the
base. (An explanatory booklet on degree days and how to use them is published by the Department
of Energy as Number 7 in the Fuel Efficiency Booklet series.) Lack of correlation between fuel
consumption and the degree day series is likely to signify poor heating control.

Electricity Consumption and Charges

Electricity is charged to the industrial and commercial customer in accordance with one of the
published tariffs of the relevant Area Board. (Only the very largest consumers can negotiate terms
outside the published lists.) For premises with a demand exceeding about 30 kW, the consumer
pays not only for units consumed but also for peaks of demand, including those caused by poor
power factor. In present day, delivered price terms electricity is close to three times the price of
premium oil products and nearly four times that of natural gas when compared on a straight
thermal content basis.

Nevertheless the use of electricity will be justified, in certain circumstances, by its inherently
more effective energy transfer, for example in induction heating, and in some forms of resistance
heating. Superior controllability and cleanliness may also confer incidental advantages of improved
productivity and product quality compared with fossil fuels.

For all these reasons careful attention must be paid to the organisation's electricity costs.
Customer tariffs, as supplied by the Area Boards, are related to the Board's own costs which, in
England and Wales, largely reflect their cost of purchase from the Central Electricity Generating
Board under the Bulk Supply Tariff.

An understanding of the alternative tariffs available is essential. It cannot be assumed that the
one providing the least overall cost is the one already in use, for electricity requirements and tariff
details may well have changed since selection was made.

Making the maximum use of off-peak facilities is important in keeping costs down. Off-peak
consumption may cost as little as half, or even one third, the normal day rate. Existing work
practices and heating requirements should therefore be examined to ensure that off-peak supplies
are used wherever advantageous.

Tariffs can be of a one-, two- or three-part nature. In the first case payment is made for units
(kilowatt-hours) of electricity used. This can be calculated on a flat rate basis where the same unit
price is charged regardless of consumption or on a descending block rate with lower prices being
progressively introduced over bands of additional consumption.

Two- (or three-) part tariffs are more common for industrial and commercial consumers. In the
case of two-part tariffs account is taken not only of the amount of units consumed but also of a
specific characteristic of that demand, normally the 'maximum demand'. (Three-part tariffs
embrace both these facets together with a service charge separately agreed and which may not
coincide with billing periods.)

Maximum demand may be measured in kilowatts (kW)—power usefully used—or in kilovolt
amperes (kVA)—the apparent power delivered. (The distinction between these two measures is
discussed later in the context of power factor improvement.) Maximum demand is the highest
average value of any 30 minute period taken over a month, a quarter or a year.

Action to avoid excessive maximum demand charges is basic to cost effective energy management. Production procedures and schedules should be examined to ensure, wherever possible, a
smooth and reasonably constant total demand profile for electricity. Maximum demand controllers
can be used to shed loads automatically when predetermined consumption rates are reached—see
Chapter 4 for a further discussion on these controls.

Another aspect of electricity consumption which must also be examined relates to the 'power
factor' of plant and equipment. This is a measure of the utilisation of the current metered to a
consumer. In certain cases, such as in resistance space heaters, the amount of power used is equal

to the product of the amperes used and the voltage of supply. In these circumstances the current is being fully utilised and the appliance is said to have a power factor of 1.0.

But in other cases, involving inductive loads, part of the current is required to magnetise the equipment without producing power or other usefully converted energy. Low power factor results in excessive current levels for the power realised with corresponding penalties on maximum demand charges.

Improvements can be made by installing power factor correction capacitors. The relationship between kilowatts (kW) and kilovolt-amperes (kVA) and the reactive, in this case inductive, component of current can be represented by a right-angled triangle—see Figure 2.2.

If any two of these quantities are measured the third can be calculated. Power factor correction capacitors work by offsetting the inductive (wattless) current reducing the angle and so reducing kVA and total current or in other words it improves the power factor. Economic power factor correction justifies the cost of the capacitors by reducing maximum demand charges.

Monitoring and Data Presentation

Weekly readings of electricity consumption, as of the other forms of energy supplied, form a reasonable base for monitoring where the cost is at all significant. Where large supplies and costs are involved continuous recording of consumption may be advisable.

Comparing weekly (or daily) energy consumption levels with an indicator of activity, possibly output, and temperature enables the effect of varying conditions on energy consumption to be seen. In this way the most economical and acceptable procedures can be identified and adopted as standard.

A simple and useful way of illustrating energy flows in terms of individual process needs and energy wastage is by means of a Sankey diagram, as illustrated in Figure 2.3. This allows the energy manager to gain an appreciation of the overall scene in his plant: the size of loads required; the roles played by each fuel; and the levels of waste attached to current practices. It also offers an easily understood way of illustrating to colleagues the amounts of energy consumed and the scope available for improving energy efficiency.

The example shown in Figure 2.3 uses energy cost rather than, say, megajoules. This stresses the high cost of electrical energy, and is probably a more realistic basis for management accounting purposes.

Finally it is important to ensure that, once instigated, measurement and monitoring practices continue. In this way a reliable record can be built up over time and the effects of individual actions can be monitored. Maintaining the interest of both workforce and managers is also vital for the energy manager if he is to retain the support he requires. Lapsed systems are normally associated with lost causes.

Case Study of an Industrial Energy Survey

The company manufactures chemicals and the plant is located in northern England. It uses one fuel only, natural gas, for all its heating needs including direct fired applications and steam raising for both process and space heating. The plant has developed over the years and the heating methods have been modified to take advantage of the more recently available natural gas supply.

Gas oil was formerly the principal fuel. It was used for the direct-fired calcining kilns, and for the steam boiler which met all other process loads as well as the space heating. The kilns and boiler have been converted to natural gas firing as has the warm air heating in the warehouse.

The original extensive steam distribution system remains and operates 168 hours a week mainly for one continuous process, the tin plant, and for some minor space heating and frost protection measures. There is one packaged steam boiler, which is 16 years old and formerly rated at 6,900 lbs per hour. It is larger than the present maximum load and gives frequent trouble from tube leakage.

FIGURE 2.2: REACTIVE CURRENT AND THE POWER FACTOR

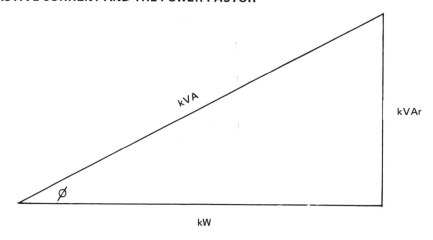

FIGURE 2.3: A SANKEY DIAGRAM

The example relates to a Sand Quarry

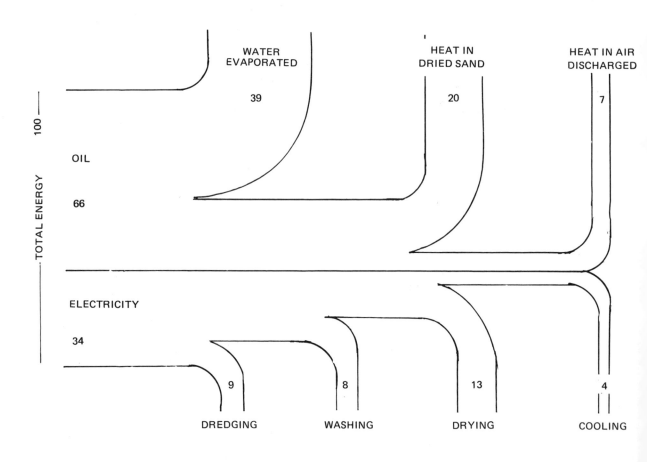

*Figures Represent Per Cent
of Total Energy Cost*

There is only one gas meter for the total site and no monitoring had been carried out. Gas bills were, however, available showing a present rate of annual consumption of 251,000 therms equivalent, at current prices, to £81,324 a year.

No indication of steam consumption was available either but plant loadings were established and these are set out in Table 2.4.

Survey Approach and Procedure

Having established what data there was available the next stage in the exercise was to break down the total site gas consumption into the several elements of direct fired plant and the steam applications for process and space heating. These consumptions could then be compared with the estimated requirements of each load and any discrepancies could be examined.

Assessing Plant Energy Consumption

In the absence of internal metering frequent readings of the main gas meter were taken on four days spanning a full week in January. The meter was read at the beginning and end of each working day and at approximate hourly intervals between.

Gas consumptions for various combinations of heating loads were thereby determined and condensate tests and steam heating calculations were used to account for the steam output of the boiler. In this way a reasonably approximate breakdown of fuel use by load could be established.

These rates of inferred consumption are given in Table 2.5. Gas consumption of the steam heated items was inferred from the increase in boiler gas consumption arising from any item. The inferred consumption for individual items was arrived at with the help of the following observations, tests and calculated estimates:

- the boiler on testing showed a 66 per cent efficiency at one third MCR

- the warehouse heating was found to be on continuously at maximum during the day due to excessive ventilation and stratification problems

- a condensate test on the tin plant showed steam consumption at 80 lbs per hour in line with the calculated heat loss from this low temperature reaction vessel

- a condensate test on the dryer showed steam consumption at 380 lbs per hour which gave a ratio of 3.6 lbs of steam per lb of moisture evaporated, not too bad a performance for a difficult drying process

- the office heating estimate was based on heat loss calculations for the office block

- steam consumptions for heating in the canteen, B shop and works were calculated as heat emissions of the measured panels and coils.

Allowing for the varying seasonal, weekly and daily load factors—the production plant operates eight hours a day for five days a week and the heating plant is switched off in the summer—a weighted consumption analysis was arrived at.

This is shown in Table 2.6 and gives an estimated annual gas consumption figure of 260,267 therms, in close comparison with the 251,000 therms metered.

Survey Findings

Amongst the many possible improvements Table 2.6 clearly shows the outstanding opportunity for reducing the sizable steam boiler and distribution losses.

The only steam load essential at nights and weekends is in the tin plant and this could be carried by suitable immersion heating, in this case electric immersion heaters of 23.4 kW capacity.

TABLE 2.4: LOADING OF PROCESS AND SPACE HEATING PLANT

Hours per week

Direct gas fired

Steam boiler, 6,900 lbs per hour MCR	168
Two kilns, maximum burner ratings, 6 therms per hour each	126
Warm air heating to warehouse, 8 units x 100,000 Btus per hour output each	60.5

Steam heated

Product dryer	50
Tin plant	168
Space heating, office block, wet system	77
Space heating, canteen, wet system	112
Space heating, B shop—radiant panels	168
Space heating, works—radiant panels	168

No indication of steam consumptions available

TABLE 2.5: INFERRED GAS CONSUMPTION BY PROCESS AND LOAD

	Equipment on(*) / off(−) at time of meter reading					Inferred Consumption
(Reading	*I*	*II*	*III*	*IV*	*V*)	*(Therms per hour)*
Kiln A	*	*	*	−	−	4
Kiln B	½	−	−	−	−	4
Warehouse heating	*	−	*	*	−	10
Boiler and distribution loss	*	*	*	*	*	21
Tin plant	*	*	*	*	*	1
Dryer	*	−	*	*	−	5
Space heating office	*	−	*	*	−	4
Space heating canteen	*	*	*	*	*	0.5
Space heating B shop	*	*	*	*	*	1
Space heating works	*	*	*	*	*	1.5
Metered therms per hour	50	29	48	44	25	

TABLE 2.6: ESTIMATED GAS CONSUMPTION BY PROCESS AND LOAD

Item	Hours	Days	Weeks	Factor	Therms per hour	Therms per year	Percentage of total
1½ kilns	24	5	49		6	35,280	13.6
Warehouse heating	11	5.5	35	0.6	10	12,705	4.9
Boiler and distribution losses	24	7	49		21	172,872	66.4
Tin plant	24	7	49		1	8,232	3.2
Dryer	10	5	49		5	12,250	4.7
Office space heating	11	7	35	0.6	4	6,468	2.5
Canteen space heating	16	7	32		0.5	1,792	0.7
B shop space heating	24	7	32		1	5,376	2.1
Works space heating	24	7	35	0.6	1.5	5,292	2.0
Total						260,267	100

With very minor provision of local heating–gas radiant panels were proposed–steam raising for space heating could also be eliminated at nights and weekends and the boiler shut down for 108 hours a week. Further fuel savings would result if it were possible to eliminate the steam boiler.

The annual savings that could be expected from curtailing the use of the boiler and its eventual elimination were calculated and these appear in Tables 2.7 and 2.8.

TABLE 2.7: CALCULATED NET ANNUAL SAVINGS FROM CURTAILING BOILER USE AT NIGHTS AND WEEKENDS

Annual saving by reduced boiler hours 108 x 49 x 21 therms x 32.4 p/therm	36,006
Extra cost of continuous electric heating of Tin Plant 23.4 kW x 8232 h x 3.4p/kWh	6,549
Allow annual cost for local heating (gas)	400
Allow annual charge for capital cost	500
Net annual saving from stopping boiler at nights and weekends	£28,557

TABLE 2.8: CALCULATED NET ANNUAL SAVINGS FROM REPLACING BOILER WITH NEW DIRECT FIRED PLANT

	Annual therms of gas		
		Saved from boiler	*Required by new plant*
New direct gas fired dryer		12,250	12,000
Gas boiler for office wet system		6,468	6,000
Gas radiant heating for B shop		5,376	2,000
Gas radiant heating for works		5,292	3,000
Gas radiant heating for canteen		1,792	1,000
Boiler and distribution loss 60h x 49 weeks x 21 therm		61,740	
Total saved		92,981	less 24,000
Less new usage		24,000	
Net therms saved		68,981	
Value of saving at 32.4 pence per therm		22,350	
Less allowance for capital charges		5,600	
Net extra annual saving from elimination of steam boiler		£16,750	

Recommendations

These findings were accepted by the company's management and the reduction in boiler firing has already taken place. The full summary of the main recommendations resulting from the survey, some of which were mutually exclusive, together with their annual fuel cost savings are as follows:

1. Provide alternative heating of tin plant liquor and discontinue night time and weekend steam generation (approximate annual saving £28,500)

2. Attention to improving boiler efficiency (£3,500 saving)

3. Consider stopping central steam generation (£16,700 saving)

4. Improve effectiveness of energy monitoring with involvement of
    production management

5. Locate and repair faulty steam traps then improve lagging of
    condensate return/collection system   (£2,500 saving)

6. Lag all remaining steam mains after removal of redundant lengths

7. Close warehouse doors, overcome temperature stratification (high level fans)
    and secure thermostats from interference   (£1,500 saving)

8. Control B Shop steam heating   (£1,000 saving)

9. Improve sectional valving of steam distribution system

10. Seven-day timer for office heating control   (£500 saving)

11. Attention, for electrical savings, to loading and maintenance of plant;
    install temporary load recorder   (£1,000 saving)

Taken together these savings amount to £55,200 a year. Lack of funds may allow for only a staged introduction of these measures but the survey has established the scale of savings and the priority that should be afforded to each of these measures.

3
PREPARING THE CASE FOR INVESTMENT

J. Barry Healey

This chapter sets out to provide energy managers and engineers with an appreciation of the general principles behind the financial evaluation of investment projects. It also contains a framework to follow for carrying out prima facie evaluations of energy investment projects.

It should be remembered, however, that financial analysis is a complex area and, whilst an understanding of these principles will assist the energy manager in his day-to-day work, the evaluation of all but the simplest projects should be checked with, or carried out by, an experienced accountant especially with regard to taxation implications.

The Objective of Financial Appraisal

The financial appraisal of investment projects can be defined as the process of evaluating and determining the profitability of projects involving investment and expenditure in order to make savings or obtain income.

Profitability is the key word in this definition because financial appraisal is not concerned with assessing technical feasibility but with evaluating in money terms the effect of an investment project on the future profitability of the organisation.

Businesses exist to make profits and so, from a business point of view, an investment project is only worth undertaking if it helps to meet the profit objectives. The objective of financial appraisal, therefore, is to maximise profitability by investing funds in the ways that provide the best rates of return.

Factors Influencing Financial Evaluation

The following factors will affect the financial appraisal of any project:

   —its costs, both capital and revenue, and their value and timing

   —the savings and income from the project, both capital and revenue, and their value and timing

   —the sources and costs of the funds to be invested

   —taxation

   —inflation, and

   —risk and uncertainty.

Each of these factors will be considered separately but an understanding of the effects of time is very important to this type of evaluation. Income and savings obtained now are clearly worth more than those received in the future. The earlier that income and savings can be gained the better. Conversely expenditure incurred today costs more, in terms of financing and lost opportunity costs, than expenditure incurred in the future. The later that expenditure and costs are incurred the better. With interest at ten per cent per annum for example, £100 received or spent in three years' time is equivalent to only £75 today and £62 in respect of a five year period.

Costs of the Project

To ascertain precisely what a proposed project will cost is not as easy as it might seem as there are a number of complicating factors. Firstly it is important to differentiate between *capital expenditure and costs* and *revenue expenditure and costs.* Broadly speaking capital expenditure relates to the purchase of assets which will subsequently appear in the balance sheet. Revenue expenditure, on the other hand, is taken into the profit and loss account as deductions against trading income. Items of revenue expenditure include the costs of materials used in production, payroll costs, rent and rates, general overheads and energy costs.

The evaluation of capital expenditure and costs must, in turn, take account of both *fixed asset needs* and *current asset needs*, i.e. both the fixed and working capital. Fixed assets are those, such as land, buildings, plant and machinery, which have been acquired with a view to being used and retained in the business over a long period of time. Fixed assets will normally only be disposed of when they come to the end of their useful lives or when changed circumstances in the business no longer warrant their retention. Current assets, on the other hand, are assets held temporarily with a view to being sold at a profit or converted into cash in the normal course of trading, e.g. stock-in-trade, debtors, work-in-progress, etc.

In determining a true assessment of costs decisions must also be taken on whether to include, and to what extent, such items as:

—expenditure already incurred, e.g. research and development costs

—allocations of company overheads not directly attributable to the project itself but which could be charged against it for accounting purposes if it is implemented

—internal costs such as the time devoted by the manager and his staff in setting up and implementing the project.

It is also necessary to estimate the residual values of capital assets and their anticipated length of useful life. The method to be adopted for incorporating depreciation into the calculations should also be agreed.

Finally it must be determined whether the cost and expenditure items are 'one-off' or recurring and, if the latter, whether they are fixed or will vary. Where costs will continue over several years it is important to allow for known, or expected, future variations such as fuel cost escalation, payroll increments, etc.

And throughout all these investigations into costs it is essential to establish both their value and timing in terms of when they will be incurred.

Savings and Income

As with costs and expenditure it is also necessary to distinguish between *capital savings* and *revenue savings and income* and to identify in all cases their values and timings. Examples of capital savings are the release of premises for sale, the reduction of inventory and the disposal of plant and machinery. Revenue savings and income improvements come from increased sales and also lower operating and manufacturing costs, lower mannings and reduced overheads.

Savings of an 'in-company' nature, involving perhaps the internal transfer of funds within the enterprise itself, are not normally included. Unless in exceptional circumstances, savings and income should be calculated on the basis of benefits obtained vis-a-vis the outside world.

As with costs, the estimates of savings which continue over a period of years may also be subject to variation with time. For example, a reduction now in fuel consumption and manning levels—with savings being achieved in real terms—will be worth more in money terms as time progresses as a result of fuel price escalation and payroll increments.

Sources and Costs of the Funds to be Invested

There are three possible sources of funds available for investment in a project. Whichever is used, or the mix of any combination, will determine the cost of providing these funds.

One possible source is finance already available in the enterprise, e.g. reserves built up by the retention of past profits. This is a relatively scarce commodity in these recessionary times and the finance may need to be borrowed from external sources, such as banks and finance houses, possibly in conjunction with the issue of debentures. The final avenue to raising finance is through the issue of additional shares, or stock, in the enterprise. (A fourth option for acquiring the equipment, that of leasing is discussed separately in the next section.)

How much the finance costs will depend on the source selected. In the first case of using the enterprise's own funds then the rate of return from the proposed project must at least equal the return currently being obtained on existing investments. Otherwise the impact of the new project would be to lower the average rate of return for the enterprise as a whole.

In the case of borrowed funds it will clearly be necessary to ensure that the rate of return from the project is superior to the costs of these external funds. Whilst in the final case the rate of return must at least pay for the additional servicing charges on the capital being raised and should ideally match, or improve on, the existing rate of return on investment being enjoyed by the enterprise assuming that this is higher than the capital servicing rate.

The source of capital to fund a proposed project, and hence the appropriate financing charge to be applied, will depend upon: the nature, size and timescale of the project; the availability of capital; future possible capital needs; and the enterprise's taxation plans.

Leasing

Many organisations are, however, reluctant to apply capital resources to investment projects such as the installation of energy-saving equipment and will only do so where rapid payback can be expected. It may be that the enterprise's capital resources are fully committed for essential asset replacement and for working capital commitments. Resources may simply not be available for non-essential, albeit profitable, investments.

Furthermore many organisations are simply not sufficiently profitable to take full advantage of the 100 per cent first year tax allowances on capital expenditure thus, as discussed in the following section, delaying the payback and reducing the internal rate of return.

In these circumstances leasing the equipment required may well offer many advantages. Firstly, of course, it avoids tying up capital resources and the lease can also include associated charges i.e.

—the cost of clearing and disposing of old equipment

—site clearance and preparation including civil engineering work and the provision of services

—the cost of installing the plant and machinery required for the project, and

—professional fees for consultants, etc and the costs of project management.

Moreover some projects, including those for energy-saving, may well be self-financing from the outset when leasing is involved. Such projects have annual savings exceeding the total annual leasing payments although leasing contracts can be structured to fit a lessee's, or project's, particular circumstances.

Allowing for fuel price escalation net benefits per annum will increase during the leasing period thereby improving the annual benefit gained.

Leasing payments are deductible in full for corporation tax assessment purposes. Moreover grant benefits are also available: development grants being paid to the lessor and passed on to the lessee in the form of reduced charges; and fuel conversion grants going direct to the lessee-user.

Satisfactory creditworthiness and a sound, viable project will need to be demonstrated but otherwise the leasing option is open to all organisations.

Taxation

Taxation can materially affect the viability of a project in a number of ways. Tax allowances, for example, are generated by project expenditure (of both a capital and revenue nature). These can be offset against the tax liabilities of the enterprise as a whole as well as for the project under consideration. Of major importance to the attractiveness of any project, therefore, will be the current profitability of the enterprise. It may, for example, be in a position where it is unable to take full advantage of allowances generated by the project until such time as the additional benefits generated by this or other projects enable it to do so which perhaps could be in several years time.

It should also be remembered that savings and income generated by an investment project in turn create tax liabilities. To the extent that these liabilities cannot be offset by the allowances on project expenditure, as discussed above, then the tax liability of the enterprise as a whole will be increased.

Moreover the benefit, in cash flow terms, arising from tax allowances generated by project expenditure will not normally be obtained for at least one year after that expenditure was incurred. In the same way any additional tax liability, arising as a result of project savings or income, will normally have to be paid one year after the savings or income were generated. In short, the benefits and penalties from taxation usually arise one year later than the expenditure or income transactions which give rise to them.

Inflation

The effects of timing on costs and savings have already been shown to exert an important influence on a project's profitability. The impact of a higher-than-average increase in one item's price, such as fuel price escalation, has also been noted. But whether allowance should be made for the effects of inflation in a financial assessment is open to argument.

On the one hand there is no doubt that continuing inflation will, as time goes by, increase the future financial benefits and costs arising from the implementation of a project. As noted in the previous section, if the continuing benefits from a project exceed its costs then the rate of return on the initial investment is likely to be effectively increased by inflation. And there is no doubt that provided a reasonably accurate allowance for inflation can be incorporated the resulting assessment is likely to reflect more closely the eventual financial outcome.

On the other hand it is not easy to provide a reasonably accurate allowance for inflation. Complications abound and the failure to foresee and evaluate them with even a modest degree of accuracy can result in an assessment which is invalid as a prognosis of financial viability.

The more significant complications are:

—it is not normally possible to predict the rate of inflation with an acceptable degree of accuracy beyond one, or at the most two, years

—inflation does not necessarily affect all savings and cost factors in the same way and to apply a blanket rate to all factors can be equally unrealistic

—the timings of cash inflows and outflows arising from savings and costs may differ in practice from those forecast. If so the effects of inflation would be different from any that were anticipated at the beginning of the project thereby making the initial calculations invalid.

Possibly the most prudent approach is to recognise that fixed asset replacement, if required, will be at a figure higher than the original purchase price and to make suitable allowance. Adjustment should also be made where one particular element, such as fuel cost, has, and is likely to continue, to vary from the general inflation rate and where this element exerts an important influence within the cost mix.

Otherwise it is probably best to ignore inflation in the evaluation with any favourable outcome from rising prices seen merely as a fortuitous financial bonus. A second principle to adopt is that a project's viability must be in doubt if it cannot be justified on its inherent benefits alone ignoring the effects of inflation.

Risk and Uncertainty

Statistical and analytical methods are available for appraising risk which can be used in the comparison and evaluation of projects. These methods, however, lie outside the scope of this chapter and for the present it is probably sufficient to recognise that:

- —uncertainties usually exist in the forecasts of costs and savings and realistic allowances should be made for them if at all possible
- —the longer the time-span of the project and the further into the future the forecasts are made, the greater will become the degree of risk and uncertainty.

Checklists of Costs and Savings

Tables 3.1 and 3.2 contain checklists of the headings under which costs can be incurred and savings obtained as a result of implementing capital projects.

In any given project appraisal all relevant cost and savings factors need to be identified and assessed. In this case items within the tables most likely to apply in energy conservation projects have been asterisked.

The Cash Flow Statement

A prerequisite to any financial appraisal must be the preparation of a statement, in as much detail as is reasonably appropriate, for each project under examination. The statement should include:

- —the values and timings of all funds to be applied and the costs to be incurred
- —the values and timings of all savings to be made and income to be received.

A specimen form of cash flow statement for an investment project is to be found in Table 3.3. This relates to an installation of new heat treatment furnaces with automatic temperature and environmental controls in order to save fuel, reduce the need for operator intervention and improve product quality, thereby leading to higher sales.

It is conventional practice to show the initial one-off costs and savings as being incurred or gained in 'year 0' with recurring costs and savings commencing in 'year 1'. If however a project results in further one-off costs and savings during its life these should be included in the year in which they are expected to arise.

The number of years over which a project is evaluated is usually determined by the expected useful life of the assets employed. In other words it will conform to the number of years over which the assets will be depreciated to a residual book value or to zero.

It will be seen from the table that no account has yet been taken of taxation implications nor of possible variations in costs and savings. These are the subjects to which we now turn.

The Effects of Taxation on Cash Flow

Returning to the initial cash flow statement in Table 3.3 the likely effects of taxation can now be identified. The standard rate of Corporation Tax for medium and larger companies is 52 per cent; allowing for the twelve month time lag the savings in year 0 of £60,000 result in an additional tax charge in year 1 of £31,000 as shown in Table 3.4. Similarly the savings achieved in year 1 of £170,000 result in a tax charge in year 2 of £88,000 and so on. These figures must then be added to the total costs to arrive at the total outflow.

Now the tax implications on the increased expenditure must be taken into account and for the purposes of the worked example the full 100 per cent first year tax allowance has been assumed on the capital expenditure items whilst the revenue cost items appearing under running costs

TABLE 3.1: CHECKLIST OF COSTS

Land and Building Costs

Purchase, site clearance, provision of access and
  workroads
Alterations, extensions, civil engineering work ●
Provision of services and associated control
  systems: air-conditioning, heating, lighting,
  plumbing, air, gas, fluids, supply, waste disposal
  and general drainage ●
Partitioning, insulation (noise and/or heat,
  vibration and draughts), decoration, floor
  covering and treatment ●
Fixtures and fittings, furnishings ●
Fire prevention, e.g. sprinkler systems ●
Environmental controls ●
Use of temporary premises ●
Security systems ●
Disposal costs: dilapidations, renovations, book
  value write-offs, site clearance
Professional Charges: agents' fees and costs,
  solicitors' fees and costs, architects' fees and
  costs, consultants' fees and costs ●
Hire of special equipment ●
Depreciation costs ●
Rent and rates

Plant and Machinery Costs

Purchase or leasing costs ●
Site preparation, civil engineering work ●
Provision of services, associated processes ●
Installation costs ●
Dismantling, renovation, relocation ●
Hire of special equipment ●
Retooling
Maintenance charges ●
Depreciation costs ●
Machine utilisation and downtime ●
Professional charges ●
Provision of safety systems ●
Insulation, i.e. noise, vibration, heat etc ●
NBV write-offs in event of disposal ●

Working Capital Costs

Increased inventory values: raw materials,
  consumables, components, assemblies, finished
  stocks
Inventory write-offs
Increased work-in-progress levels, debtor levels
Increase in provision for bad and doubtful debts
Stockholding and financing charges
Space requirements, fixtures and fittings for
  inventory and work-in-progress
Transport and/or relocation of inventories

Personnel Costs

Redundancy payments ●
Payments in lieu of notice ●
Retention incentive payments
Productivity bonus payments
Overtime payments
Shift and working conditions premium payments
Salary and wage costs and related overheads ●
Changes to remuneration systems
Changes in working practices ●
Use of contract labour
Use of temporaries
Replacement costs
Relocation costs
Training costs ●
Travelling and accommodation charges
Special clothing
Time recording systems

Business Disruption/Protection Costs

Temporary build-up of inventories
Extended supply/manufacturing lead-times
Increased work-in-progress
Use of alternative sourcing
Loss of sales during changeover
Narrowing of profit margins
Reduced customer service levels
Fall in process yields and/or productivity
Materials wastage
Shortfall of skills availability
Publicity measures
Security measures

Other Potential Cost Factors

Market research work
Feasibility studies, pilot studies ●
Project planning and control ●
Transitional control systems ●
Changes to management and administrative
  systems and procedures
Promotion and publicity costs
Design work
Patenting of new products
Transport and other costs arising from geographic
  changes
Insurances
Trade subscriptions
Stationery
Communications systems
Professional fees and costs
Taxation charges ●
Commission payments and royalties
Costs of raising capital ●
Increased production lead-times

●   *Items most likely to apply to energy conservation projects*

TABLE 3.2: CHECKLIST OF SAVINGS

Land and Buildings

Sales of land and buildings
Vacation of land and buildings (i.e. saving of
    rent and rates)
Sub-letting of land and buildings
Reduction in services costs (heating, lighting etc)●
Reduction of maintenance costs ●

Plant and Machinery

Sales of plant and machinery ●
Reduction of power and other services
    requirements●
Improved machine utilisation ●
Reduced maintenance costs ●
Increased working life, i.e. lower depreciation
Termination or reduction of leased items and
    leasing charges
Improved handling methods
Use of less expensive plant and machinery●

Working Capital

Reduced inventory values
Reduction of work-in-progress levels
Reduced debtor levels; decrease in incidence of
    bad and doubtful debts
Reduction of space and equipment requirements
    for inventories

Reduced financing charges
Improved credit terms from suppliers
Disposal of surplus stocks

Personnel

Reduction of manning levels●
Improved productivity●
Reduction of overtime
Reduction of lost time ●
Improved working conditions ●

Other

Increases in sales and/or profit margins●
Grants, subsidies ●
Increased tax allowances ●
Improved process yields ●
Reduced packing and transport costs
Improved lead-times and/or customer service levels
Improved quality ●
Insurances
Trade subscriptions
Stationery
Communications
Geographic factors
Savings of scale
Marketing and sales considerations

●   *Items most likely to apply to energy conservation projects*

will also claim full relief as part of revenue expenditure. In this way the allowance of 52 per cent against tax can be calculated and this added to the total savings to show total inflows.

A comparison at this stage between Tables 3.3 and 3.4 shows the major effect taxation has had cutting the net cash flow forecasts by more than half from £465,000 to £224,000, ample demonstration that taxation simply cannot be ignored when producing an initial project cash flow whether it be for energy-saving or any other investment.

The Effects of Fuel Price Escalation

Reference has been made earlier in this chapter to the important effects cost escalation can have on cash flow particularly when one factor of significance within the overall calculation increases in price at a consistently higher than average rate. Fuel prices clearly form one such group having over the last three years risen in real terms by over 40 per cent.

Table 3.5 demonstrates the effect of fuel price escalation, taken at 10 per cent per annum compound in real terms, over the project's life. Here it can be seen that the total savings figures rise steadily from year 2 onwards although part of this gain to the enterprise is clawed back through higher tax on these savings.

Principal Methods of Financial Appraisal

Suitably armed with a reliable cash flow statement based on a full and realistic assessment of the costs and savings involved the point has now been reached where the project can be appraised for its financial merits: in short to determine whether it is worth carrying out.

TABLE 3.3: A SPECIMEN CASH FLOW STATEMENT

Project for New Furnaces with Automated Fuel Control

Costs/Savings £000 Year	0	1	2	3	4	5	Total
Implementation Costs							
Feasibility study	5						
Site clearance & preparation	15						
Electrics & cabling	15						
New plant	90						
Control hardware	65						
Terminals	40						
Purchase of software	20						
Operator retraining	5						
Recruitment costs	5						
Miscellaneous	10						
Running Costs							
Additional maintenance		5	5	5	5	5	
Control engineers		25	25	25	25	25	
Miscellaneous		5	5	5	5	5	
Total costs	270	35	35	35	35	35	
Tax on savings							
Total Cash Outflow	270	35	35	35	35	35	-445
Savings							
Sale of old plant	10						
Grants	50						
Reduced manning		50	50	50	50	50	
Fuel savings		70	70	70	70	70	
Profit on inc. sales		50	50	50	50	50	
Total savings	60	170	170	170	170	170	
Tax allowances							
Total Cash Inflow	60	170	170	170	170	170	+910
NET CASH FLOW	(210)	135	135	135	135	135	+465

TABLE 3.4: EFFECTS OF TAXATION ON CASH FLOW

Cashflow £000 Year	0	1	2	3	4	5	6	Total
Total costs	270	35	35	35	35	35		
Tax on savings		31	88	88	88	88	88	
Total Outflow	270	66	123	123	123	123	88	
Total savings	60	170	170	170	170	170		
Tax allowances		140	18	18	18	18	18	
Total Inflow	60	310	188	188	188	188	18	
NET CASH FLOW	(210)	244	65	65	65	65	(70)	+224

TABLE 3.5: EFFECT OF FUEL PRICE ESCALATION ON CASH FLOW

Escalation taken at 10 per cent per annum

Cashflow £000 Year	0	1	2	3	4	5	6	Total
Total costs	270	35	35	35	35	35		
Tax on savings	31	88	92	96	100	105	105	
Total Outflow	270	66	123	127	131	135	105	
Total savings	60	170	177	185	193	202		
Tax allowances		140	18	18	18	18	18	
Total Inflow	60	310	195	203	211	220	18	
NET CASH FLOW	(210)	244	72	76	80	85	(87)	+260

There are three principal methods of financial appraisal two of which have their own variations, viz:

—the payback period approach to identify how quickly the investment can be recouped through increased savings

—the accounting rate of return to show the expected profit as a percentage of the investment required: this being given either as the average gross or average net annual rate of return, and

—the discounted cash flow approach using either net present values or an internal rate of return.

The above methods can apply to all forms of project no matter what their purpose. As far as investment in energy-saving projects is concerned the results expected to flow back over a period of time can be assessed in all these ways albeit, as we shall see, with different results.

The Payback Method

This is the simplest method of appraisal involving nothing more than calculating the time required to recover the initial capital outlay or, in other words, how long it will take for the investment to pay for itself.

Table 3.6 shows three alternative projects, each involving a capital outlay of £100,000 although with very different cash inflow expectations. The payback period is found by straight-line interpolation of the cumulative cash flow in the year in which the break even point is reached and passed. The cash flows and results are shown in graphic form in Figure 3.7.

TABLE 3.6: THE PAYBACK METHOD OF FINANCIAL APPRAISAL

Year	Project A Net Cash Flow* £		Project B Net Cash Flow £		Project C Net Cash Flow £	
	Per Annum	Cumulative	Per Annum	Cumulative	Per Annum	Cumulative
0	(100,000)	(100,000)	(100,000)	(100,000)	(100,000)	(100,000)
1	50,000	(50,000)	10,000	(90,000)	36,000	(64,000)
2	45,000	(5,000)	15,000	(75,000)	36,000	(28,000)
3	30,000	25,000	50,000	(25,000)	36,000	8,000
4	30,000	55,000	50,000	25,000	36,000	44,000
5	20,000	75,000	70,000	95,000	36,000	80,000
	Payback	2.2 years	Payback	3.5 years	Payback	2.8 years

* Net cash flow is normally defined as profit after tax but without charging depreciation.

FIGURE 3.7: THE PAYBACK PERIOD METHOD—CUMULATIVE CASH INFLOWS

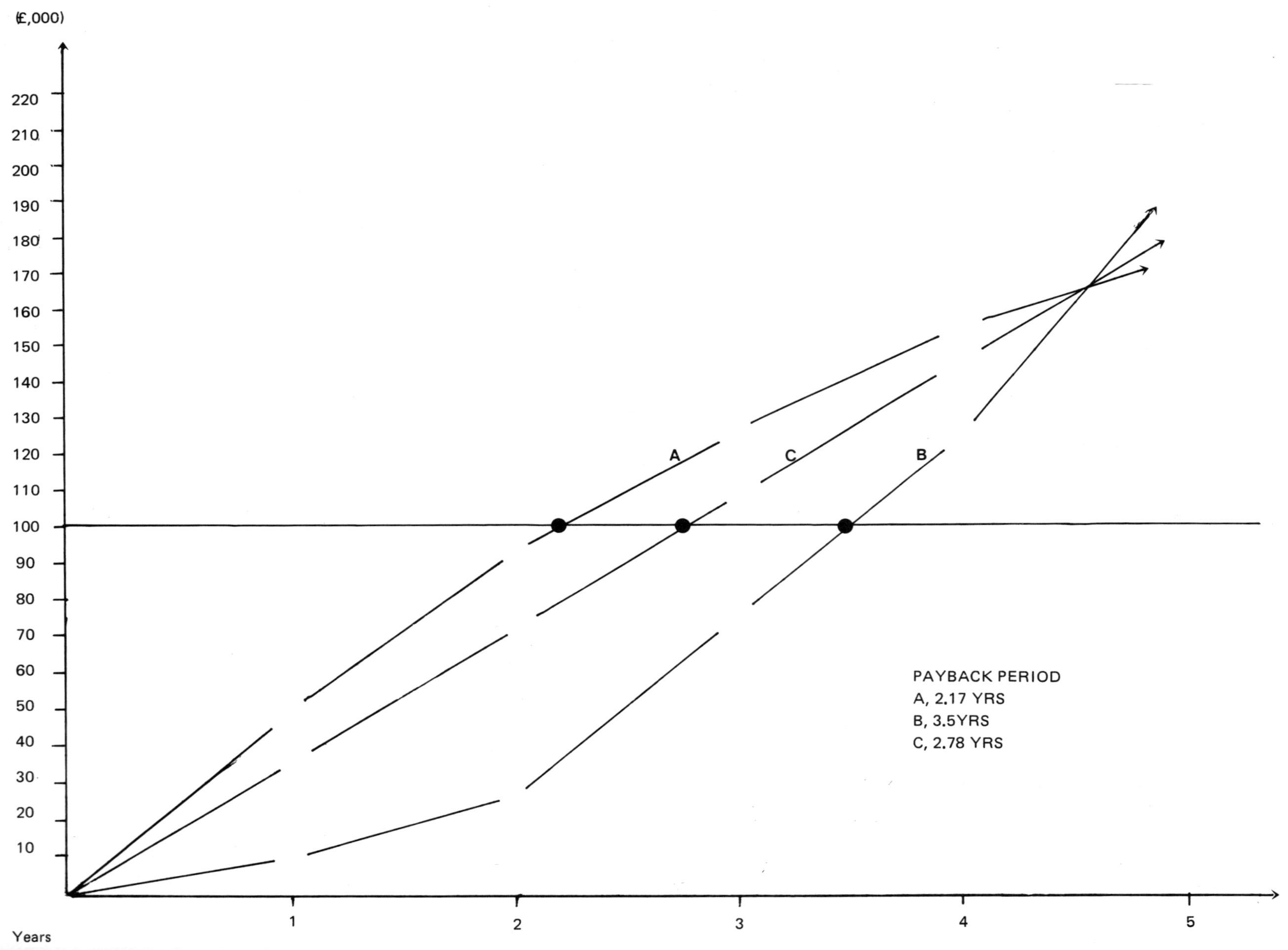

(£,000)

220
210
200
190
180
170
160
150
140
130
120
110
100
90
80
70
60
50
40
30
20
10

1   2   3   4   5

Years

A

C

B

PAYBACK PERIOD
A, 2.17 YRS
B, 3.5YRS
C, 2.78 YRS

The payback period approach has certain advantages. It is easy to understand and simple to work out. It emphasises the importance of cash-flow as a dominant factor and it is biased against long term projects where risk and uncertainty, e.g. about inflation, are more significant.

But there are disadvantages. It ignores income arising after the payback period and the timing of cash flows from the point of view of cost of funds. It cannot show the rate of return on the investment, i.e. its profitability and it ignores the earning life and residual value of the assets employed.

For these reasons adopting the payback approach is likely to prove an insufficient and imprecise tool for appraisal purposes.

The Accounting Rate of Return

This method is sometimes also known as the average annual rate of return on investment. And whilst the payback method was concerned entirely with cash flow and with no measure of profitability, this approach concentrates conversely on profitability and takes no account of cash flow.

It does take into account earnings over the entire life span of the project but does not take into account the timing of those earnings i.e. it assumes that all money is of equal value no matter when it is spent or received.

There are two basic variants to this method:

—the average *gross* annual rate of return

—the average *net* annual rate of return.

These are now considered separately.

Average Gross Annual Rate of Return is defined as the average proceeds per year over the life of the assets expressed as a percentage of the original capital cost. Table 3.8 returns to the three alternatives analysed by payback in Table 3.6. This shows that project B, the one previously assessed with the longest payback, now appears the most attractive.

TABLE 3.8: THE AVERAGE GROSS RATE OF RETURN APPROACH

£	Project A	B	C
Total net cash inflow	175,000	195,000	180,000
Average net cash inflow per annum	35,000	39,000	36,000
Average gross return (Capital cost = £100,000 in each case)	35%	39%	36%

Capital cost is the total cost incurred or estimated for putting the assets into a revenue-earning position. For new plant this would include the purchase price and installation costs plus any additional working capital requirements

Total net cash inflow is the excess, for the total life of the project, of total revenue over total costs excluding depreciation and ignoring the effect of taxation.

Average Net Annual Rate of Return is defined as the average proceeds per year, after allowing for depreciation over the life of the assets expressed as a percentage of the average value of the capital employed. Table 3.9 uses the same examples as above and the results are once again charted in graphical form in Figure 3.10.

TABLE 3.9: THE AVERAGE NET ANNUAL RATE OF RETURN APPROACH

£	Project A	B	C
Total net cash inflow	175,000	195,000	180,000
Less depreciation	(100,000)	(100,000)	(100,000)
Net return	75,000	95,000	80,000
Average net cash inflow per annum	15,000	19,000	16,000
Average net return on average capital employed (£50,000)	30%	38%	32%

Average capital employed is usually taken as the average of the original capital cost and residual value, i.e. £50,000 in this example. Other methods, however, can be used depending, for example, on the method of depreciation adopted and on the expected residual value.

The advantages of both of the above methods are:

—they are easy to understand and compute

—they emphasise profitability as returns over the whole life of the assets are taken into account

—the concept of return on capital employed is the single most important yardstick used in the measurement of business performance.

But once again there are disadvantages. No acknowledgement can be made to the timing of costs or receipts and irregularities in the cash flow are smoothed out and once averaged no indication is given of the time-span of the return.

Discounted Cash Flow (DCF)

DCF methods of investment appraisal involve discounting future outflows and inflows of cash back to present day values thus establishing a common base for the comparison of investment alternatives.

They acknowledge the importance of timing, i.e. that funds invested in the future have less impact than funds invested now and that funds received early in a project are worth more than funds received later.

There are two basic methods of DCF assessment:

—net present value method

—internal rate of return method.

In both methods like is compared with like in that the *present value* of the funds invested is compared with the *present value* of the net cash flows expected to be generated over the life of the investment.

The financial adequacy of the investment is measured by the average effective rate of interest earned on the outstanding balances over the life of the investment. Tax payments and tax allowances are usually incorporated in the cash flow computations according to the timing when these payments and allowances have effect.

Net Present Value Method involves the discounting of future cash flows back to their present day values by using the minimum acceptable rate of return as the discounting rate.

The information required for the computation is:

—the initial cost of the project

FIGURE 3.10: ACCOUNTING RATE OF RETURN

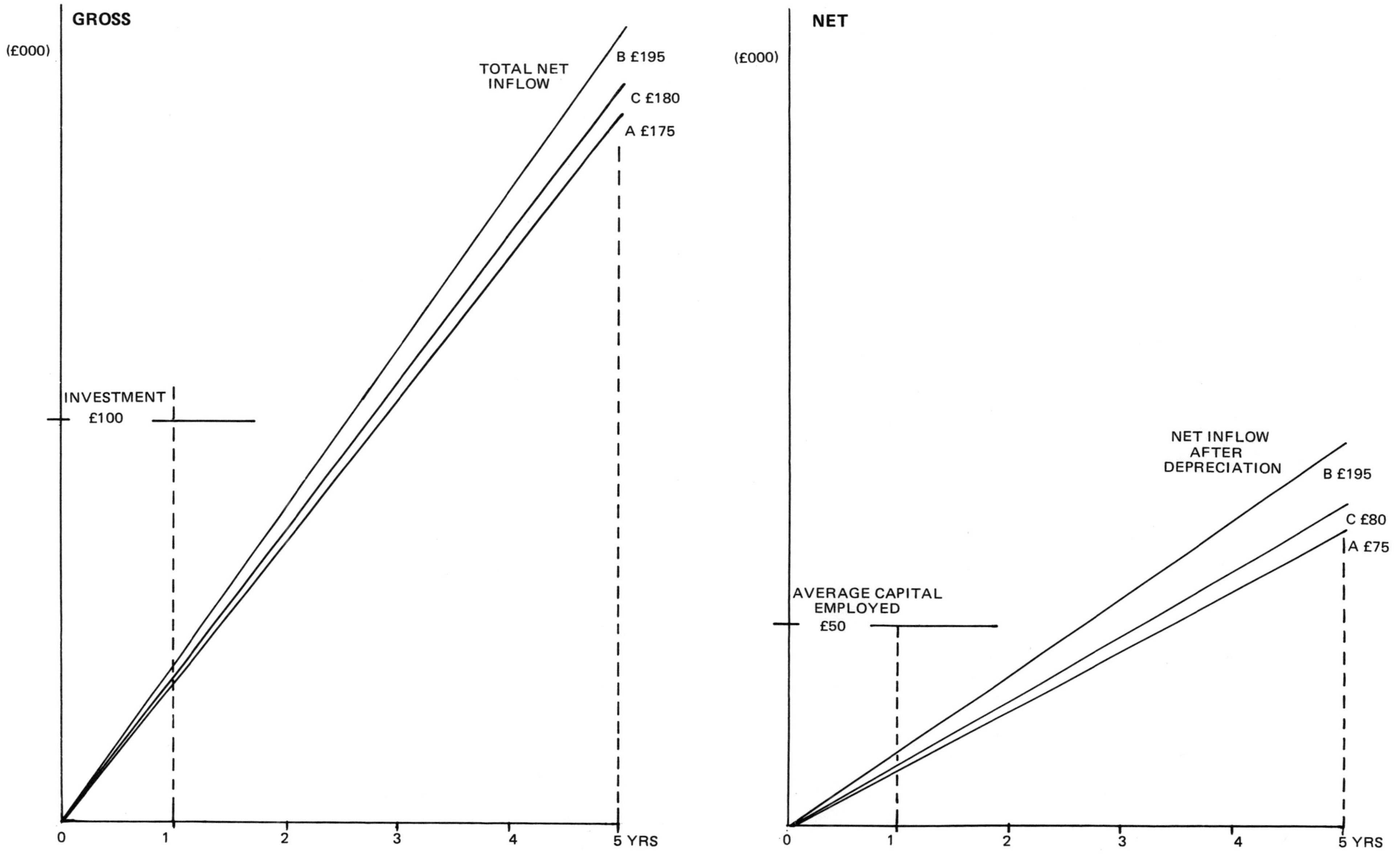

GROSS
(£000)
TOTAL NET INFLOW
B £195
C £180
A £175
INVESTMENT
£100
0
1
2
3
4
5 YRS
NET
(£000)
NET INFLOW AFTER DEPRECIATION
B £195
C £80
A £75
AVERAGE CAPITAL EMPLOYED
£50
0
1
2
3
4
5 YRS

—the cost of supplying the capital required, i.e. the minimum rate of return to be obtained from the investment

—the values and timings of future cash flows for the total expected life of the project

—a reference table of discount factors,—see Table 3.12.

The method of computation is as follows:

1. Compute the present day value of each year's cash inflow by multiplying the values of those inflows by the appropriate discount factors

2. Summate the values thus computed to give the total present day value of future cash benefits

3. Similarly compute the present day values of future cash outflows and add the sum of these present day values to the initial cost of the project

4. If the total arrived at under heading 2, i.e. the total present day value of all future returns, exceeds the total arrived at in point 3, i.e. the present day value of the investment costs, the project should be accepted and vice versa.

Where several alternative projects are being considered, the one showing the highest positive result would be the one accepted.

It can be seen in Table 3.11 that project A provides the lowest total cash inflow, has the shortest payback period and the highest return on investment where the cost of funds is 10 per cent or thereabouts.

TABLE 3.11: EXAMPLE OF NET PRESENT VALUE METHOD

Project A	£	Net Cash Flow	Discount Factor @ 10%	Present Day Value
Year 0		(100,000)	1.0000	(100,000)
1		50,000	.9091	45,455
2		45,000	.8264	37,188
3		30,000	.7513	22,539
4		30,000	.6830	20,490
5		20,000	.6209	12,418
Total Cash Flow		+£75,000		Total NPV +£38,090
Project B				
Year 0		(100,000)	1.0000	(100,000)
1		10,000	.9091	9,091
2		15,000	.8264	12,396
3		50,000	.7513	37,565
4		50,000	.6830	34,150
5		70,000	.6209	43,463
Total Cash Flow		+£95,000		Total NPV +£36,665
Project C				
Year 0		(100,000)	1.0000	(100,000)
1		36,000	.9091	32,728
2		36,000	.8264	29,750
3		36,000	.7513	27,047
4		36,000	.6830	24,588
5		36,000	.6209	22,352
Total Cash Flow		+£80,000		Total NPV +£36,465

TABLE 3.12: DISCOUNT FACTORS

Year	Percentage 1	2	3	4	5	6	7	8	9	10
1	0·990099	0·980392	0·970874	0·961538	0·952381	0·943396	0·934579	0·925926	0·917431	0·909091
2	0·980296	0·961169	0·942596	0·924556	0·907029	0·889996	0·873439	0·857339	0·841680	0·826446
3	0·970590	0·942322	0·915142	0·888996	0·863838	0·839619	0·816298	0·793832	0·772183	0·751315
4	0·960980	0·923845	0·888487	0·854804	0·822702	0·792094	0·762895	0·735030	0·708425	0·683013
5	0·951466	0·905731	0·862609	0·821927	0·783526	0·747258	0·712986	0·680583	0·649931	0·620921
6	0·942045	0·887971	0·837484	0·790315	0·746215	0·704961	0·666342	0·630170	0·596267	0·564474
7	0·932718	0·870560	0·813092	0·759918	0·710681	0·665057	0·622750	0·583490	0·547034	0·513158
8	0·923483	0·853490	0·789409	0·730690	0·676839	0·627412	0·582009	0·540269	0·501866	0·466507
9	0·914340	0·836755	0·766417	0·702587	0·644609	0·591898	0·543934	0·500249	0·460428	0·424098
10	0·905287	0·820348	0·744094	0·675564	0·613913	0·558395	0·508349	0·463193	0·422411	0·385543
11	0·896324	0·804263	0·722421	0·649581	0·584679	0·526788	0·475093	0·428883	0·387533	0·350494
12	0·887449	0·788493	0·701380	0·624597	0·556837	0·496969	0·444012	0·397114	0·355535	0·318631
13	0·878563	0·773033	0·680951	0·600574	0·530321	0·468839	0·414964	0·367698	0·326179	0·289664
14	0·869963	0·757875	0·661118	0·577475	0·505068	0·442301	0·387817	0·340461	0·299246	0·263331
15	0·861349	0·743015	0·641862	0·555265	0·481017	0·417265	0·362446	0·315242	0·274538	0·239392
16	0·852821	0·728446	0·623167	0·533908	0·458112	0·393646	0·338735	0·291890	0·251870	0·217629
17	0·844377	0·714163	0·605016	0·513373	0·436297	0·371364	0·316574	0·270269	0·231073	0·197845
18	0·836017	0·700159	0·587395	0·493628	0·415521	0·350344	0·295864	0·250249	0·211994	0·179859
19	0·827740	0·686431	0·570286	0·474642	0·395734	0·330513	0·276508	0·231712	0·194490	0·163508
20	0·819544	0·672971	0·553676	0·456387	0·376889	0·311805	0·258419	0·214548	0·178431	0·148644

Year	Percentage 11	12	13	14	15	16	17	18	19	20
1	0·900901	0·892857	0·884956	0·877193	0·869565	0·862069	0·854701	0·847458	0·840336	0·833333
2	0·811622	0·797194	0·783147	0·769468	0·756144	0·743163	0·730514	0·718184	0·706165	0·694444
3	0·731191	0·711780	0·693050	0·674972	0·657516	0·640658	0·624371	0·608631	0·593416	0·578704
4	0·658731	0·635518	0·613319	0·592080	0·571753	0·552291	0·533650	0·515789	0·498669	0·482253
5	0·593451	0·567427	0·542760	0·519369	0·497177	0·476113	0·456111	0·437109	0·419049	0·401878
6	0·534641	0·506631	0·480319	0·455587	0·432328	0·410442	0·389839	0·370432	0·352142	0·334898
7	0·481658	0·452349	0·425061	0·399637	0·375937	0·353830	0·333195	0·313925	0·295918	0·279082
8	0·433926	0·403883	0·376160	0·350559	0·326902	0·305025	0·284782	0·266038	0·248671	0·232568
9	0·390925	0·360610	0·332885	0·307508	0·284262	0·262953	0·243404	0·225456	0·208967	0·193807
10	0·352184	0·321973	0·294588	0·269744	0·247185	0·226684	0·208037	0·191064	0·175602	0·161506
11	0·317283	0·287476	0·260698	0·236617	0·214943	0·195417	0·177810	0·161919	0·147565	0·134588
12	0·285841	0·256675	0·230706	0·207559	0·186907	0·168463	0·151974	0·137220	0·124004	0·112157
13	0·257514	0·229174	0·204165	0·182069	0·162528	0·145227	0·129892	0·116288	0·104205	0·093464
14	0·231995	0·204620	0·180677	0·159710	0·141329	0·125195	0·111019	0·098549	0·087567	0·077887
15	0·209004	0·182696	0·159891	0·140096	0·122894	0·107927	0·094888	0·083516	0·073586	0·064905
16	0·188292	0·163122	0·141496	0·122892	0·105865	0·093041	0·081101	0·070776	0·061837	0·054088
17	0·169633	0·145644	0·125218	0·107800	0·092926	0·080207	0·069317	0·059980	0·051964	0·045073
18	0·152822	0·130040	0·110812	0·094561	0·080805	0·069144	0·059245	0·050830	0·043667	0·037561
19	0·137678	0·116107	0·098064	0·082948	0·070265	0·059607	0·050637	0·043077	0·036695	0·031301
20	0·124034	0·103667	0·086782	0·072762	0·061100	0·051385	0·043280	0·036506	0·030836	0·026084

Source: Capital Budgeting & Company Finance: Merrett and Sykes, Longman, 1969

If the above project were being considered by an enterprise which was currently enjoying a 25 per cent return on its capital employed and was intending to use its own funds to finance the project it would be appropriate to use a discounting factor of 25 per cent in the calculations.

On this basis the total net present values of the three projects would then become:

—Project A £3,000

—Project B (£13,400)

—Project C (£3,200)

leaving only Project A with an expected performance to warrant the investment.

Internal Rate of Return (IRR) Method is a variation of the net present value method except that it is used when the cost of supplying the capital is unknown or uncertain and it is particularly useful for indicating the most profitable of several alternative projects.

It requires the same data for the computation as does the NPV method except that one starts with an assumed 'breakeven' total net present value and then works backwards, using trial and error, to find the discount rate which, when applied to the annual cash flows, produces the breakeven result.

The discount rate thus arrived at is the internal rate of return and the project showing the highest rate is the most profitable one on this basis. These computed rates of return are then compared with the enterprise's existing rate of return on its present investments, or against the cost of providing funds, to assess whether or not the new project is worth undertaking.

Using the previous examples, it can be shown that the internal rate of return for the three projects is:

—Project A approximately 27%

—Project B approximately 20%

—Project C approximately 22.5%.

Comparison of the Net Present Value (NPV) and the Internal Rate of Return (IRR) Methods

1. Both methods indicate whether a project is acceptable or not compared with the minimum acceptable rate of return or the expected finance costs of funds applied.

2. Both methods indicate a preferential ranking of alternative projects but on the basis of cash-flow (NPV Method) or profitability (IRR Method) respectively. Remember that the higher the rate of interest applied, the less valuable are cash inflows received later and the less the impact of cash outflows incurred later.

3. The NPV method assumes that the net cash inflow generated during the course of a project can be (and is) reinvested at not less than the rate of interest used as the discount factor. The IRR method assumes that the net cash inflow generated is reinvested at the IRR.

4. The IRR method produces problems of computation where the cash flow pattern is irregular in that cash outflows occur at future times in between the normal cash inflow occasions.

5. Both methods involve an assessment of the cost to the enterprise of the capital it will use for investment. This in turn requires determination of the sources of the funds to be used.

4
HEATING CONTROLS AND BUILDING AUTOMATION SYSTEMS

Fred Ranson

The installation of automatic heating controls in replacement of manual methods of operation offer significant savings in both energy and labour. These savings have increased sharply in large buildings with the development of automation systems but the correct installation and management of less sophisticated systems continue to bring worthwhile savings to most industrial and commercial properties.

This chapter reviews the current state of the art in energy management controls starting with an outline and description of the basic elements in heating control systems and setting out a checklist of simple economy measures. The benefits of optimum start controllers are described with examples given of the financial savings achieved arising from their introduction. The chapter concludes with a discussion on the fast developing area of building automation systems: where these are appropriate to install and what functions they fulfil. A detailed case study shows how the installation of a system brought a substantial annual saving in a company's fuel bill with a payback time substantially less than two years when taking tax considerations into account.

The Principles of Heating Control

Automatic controls have always been included in properly designed building services systems, but the recent series of energy crises has led to a more formal energy conservation discipline which in turn has placed greater emphasis on the installation of cost effective control devices and systems.

The main object of heating controls is to heat only as much as is required and only when required. Maintaining temperatures above required levels incurs substantial heating penalties: two degrees extra on the space heating temperature, for example, will result in a 20 per cent increase in fuel consumption.

The basic constituents determining consumption are the load and the operating time. The load can be broken down into the temperature factor multiplied by either a quantity or rate of flow of material multiplied by either a specific quantity or a rate of flow of heat.

Of these breakdowns controls can regulate time, temperature and rates of flow either individually or in combination. Heating buildings is, therefore, a complex operation. Many items need to be taken into account such as the heat losses caused through the structure by the effects of temperature, wind, rain, etc, and the heat gains within the building produced by people, machinery, lighting, solar radiation, etc.

The accurate control of internal temperatures will need, therefore, to take all these factors into account. In manual control there would be some form of indication thermometer visible to the eye. The brain, on receiving a signal, transmits an action command to the body muscle to operate an actuator or valve to control the heat input. Automatic controls work in precisely the same way as the diagram in Figure 4.1 shows. The eye is replaced by a detector, the brain by a controller and the muscle by an actuator. Definitions of these and other terms basic to control systems are set out in Table 4.2.

FIGURE 4.1: A BASIC CONTROL SYSTEM

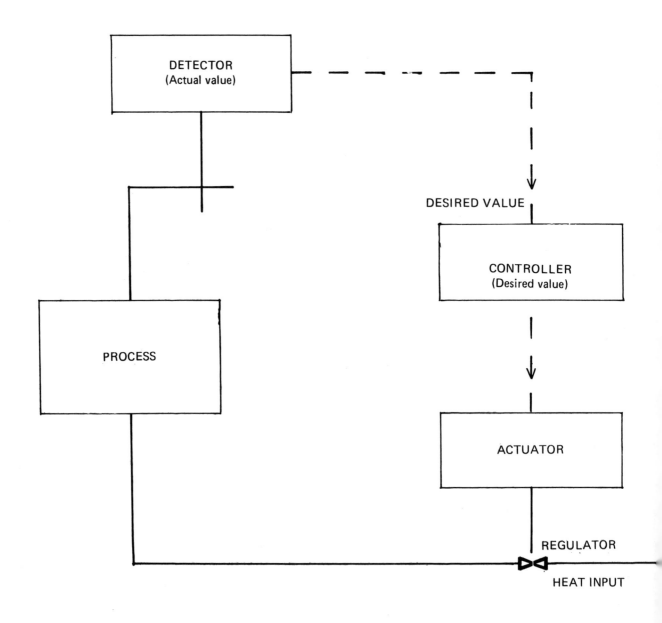

TABLE 4.2: BASIC TERMS AND ITEMS IN CONTROL SYSTEMS

1. Controlled Medium

The substance, such as air in a room, whose temperature, relative humidity or pressure etc. is being controlled and which is ultimately affected by a control agent and gains from or losses to surrounding media.

2. Variable

The temperature, relative humidity or pressure etc. to be measured or controlled.

3. Set Point

The design required value of the variable.

4. Control Point

The actual measured value of the variable.

5. Offset

The difference between the set point and the control point.

6. Detector (or Sensor or Transmitter)

The unit which transmits a signal in proportion to the value of the variable.

7. Controller

The instrument which measures one or more variables and transmits a signal in proportion to the offset.

8. Proportional Band

The change in the variable required to cause the controller to move a controlled device from one extreme limit of its travel to the other.

9. Controlled Device

The instrument which recives the controller's signal and regulates the flow of a control agent. The controlled device has two components:-

9.1 Actuator

The unit which converts the controller's signal into force to operate a regulator.

9.2 Regulator

The unit which regulates the flow of a control agent, e.g. valves, dampers.

10. Control Agent

The form of energy regulated by the control device e.g. steam, water, air, electricity.

11. Master

An instrument whose output signal is used to change the set point of a sub-master controller, e.g. manual switch, thermostat, detector, etc.

12. Distance/Velocity Lag

The elapsed time between a change in the variable and restabilisation at a new control point due to control action.

Control Devices–Valves and Dampers

It can be seen from this table that control devices have two components: the *actuator,* which converts the signal to operate the *regulator* normally a valve or damper which regulates the control agent. The final selection of valves and dampers for particular applications is a relatively complex exercise involving system pressure drops, valve and damper characterisation and pressure/flow coefficients and is best left to the experts.

It is however important to understand the basic workings of the most commonly encountered controlled devices namely three and two port valves and control dampers.

The Three Port Valve may be used in either two position or proportional control (see below) but the latter is more common, for controlling hot or chilled water flow within recirculation systems. There are two types, namely the *mixing valve* which has two inlet ports, either of which may be normally open or normally closed, and a single common outlet port, and the *diverting valve* which has two outlet ports, either of which may be normally open or normally closed, and a single common inlet port. Simple schematic representations of these are shown in Figures 4.3 and 4.4. *Mixing valves* are used to control the flow water temperature to the heating load by combining hot water from the boiler or heat source with cooler water returning after use. They involve the merging of two input sources to produce one output flow at the required temperature.

Diverting valves on the other hand operate on the principle of one inflow from the heating source and two outflows. As Figure 4.4 shows, they allow a shunt back to the boiler of the hot water which is not required.

Both valves may be installed in pipework circuits so as to effect either mixing or diverting action but it is important that flows through the valves should never be in reverse to the design directions, as this leads to leakage and damage.

In any pipework circuit the pump should always be on the common port side of the valve.

The Two Port Valve has one inlet and one outlet and is necessarily a throttling device which ultimately stops all flow. The valve may be used in either two position or proportional control and is more usually employed for controlling steam which can be shut-off completely without causing hydraulic problems. It may also be normally open or normally closed according to safety requirements in the event of control system failure.

Control Dampers may be either parallel bladed or opposed bladed, although the latter have better control characteristics, and are used for airflow control either individually or in combination.

Good control dampers are specially made for the purpose and should have minimal leakage at shut-off as well as intrinsic proportional control characteristics which are particularly important where dampers are combined for the mixing of fresh and recirculated air streams.

Control Action

The types of control action which can be employed range from simple 'on/off' to fully modulating. The initiation of any control action requires some amount of offset and the choice of the type of action depends upon the maximum offset which can be tolerated for the given application and the maximum time which can be allowed for stable conditions to be achieved.

There are five main types of control action. They are described briefly below and in diagrammatical form in Figure 4.5.

Two Position (or On/Off): once the maximum offset has been reached on one side of the set point the controlled device will be moved through its full travel and remain stationary until maximum offset is reached on the other side of the set point and so on. In this action the proportional band becomes the switching differential. An example of a simple 'on/off' control is the application to a hot water storage cylinder where the water is raised to say 45°C, the heating medium is switched off and the water allowed to drop to say 40°C before the heating medium is switched on again to repeat.

FIGURE 4.3: MIXING ACTION

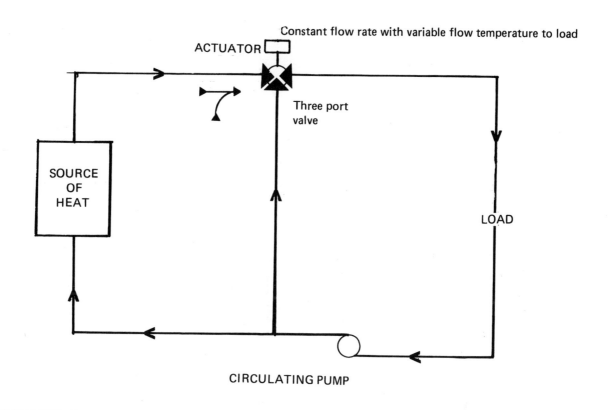

ACTUATOR

Constant flow rate with variable flow temperature to load

Three port valve

SOURCE OF HEAT

LOAD

CIRCULATING PUMP

FIGURE 4.4: DIVERTING ACTION

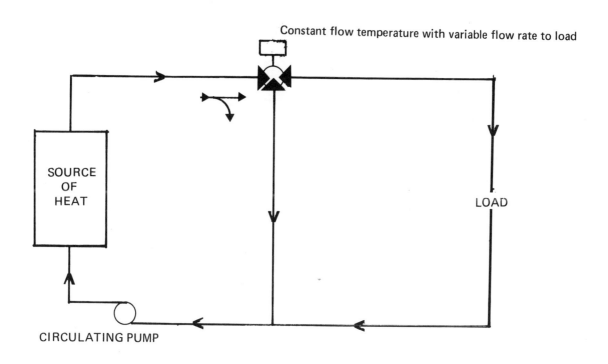

Constant flow temperature with variable flow rate to load

SOURCE OF HEAT

LOAD

CIRCULATING PUMP

FIGURE 4.5: CONTROL ACTION

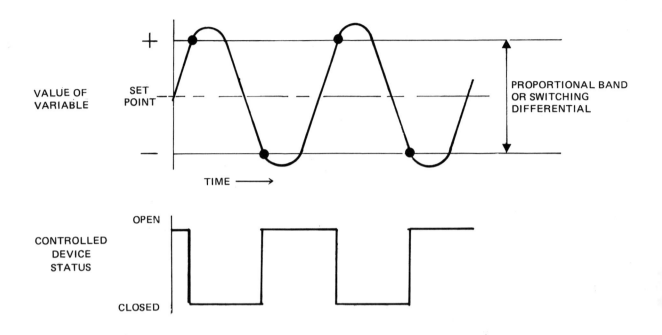

TWO POSITION ACTION

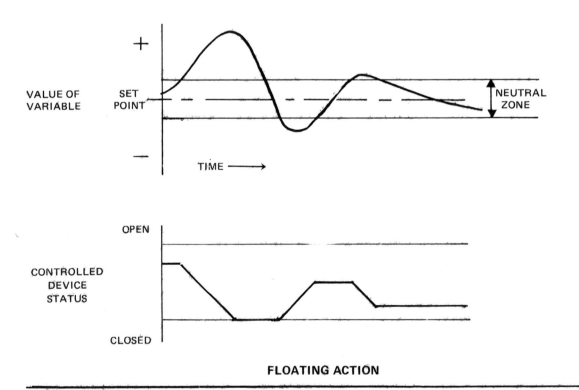

FLOATING ACTION

Figure 4.5: Control Action (Cont)

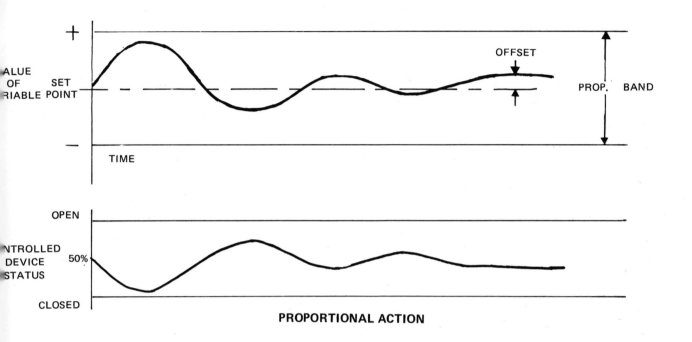

PROPORTIONAL ACTION

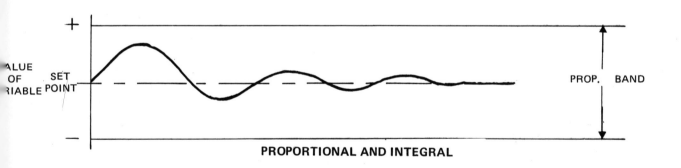

PROPORTIONAL AND INTEGRAL

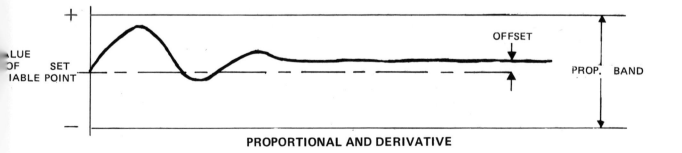

PROPORTIONAL AND DERIVATIVE

Floating Action: the controlled device is moved towards either its fully open or fully closed positions until the controller is satisfied, the limit of travel is reached or an opposite corrective movement is required. There is a neutral zone in which no movement of the controlled device is initiated.

Proportional Action: the controlled device will be fully open at one end of the proportional band, fully closed at the other end, and 50 per cent open at the set point. According to the load requirement of the controlled medium the resultant control point can be either above or below the set point but apart from when there is an exact 50 per cent load there will always be some amount of offset.

Integral Action: an additional action to proportional action where very accurate control is required. The offset is eventually reduced to zero by the controlled device being moved by increased or decreased controller signal power initiated by measurement of the offset against a time base.

Derivative Action: another additional action to proportional or proportional plus integral action where swift stabilisation of the variable is required.

The controlled device is moved by increased or decreased controller signal power initiated by measurement of the rate of change of the offset.

Two position and proportional action are by far the most commonly used in building services applications probably accounting for over 90 per cent of all installations.

Control Systems

A basic control system consists of three essential elements:

- —a controller
- —a controlled device
- —a source of power.

The controller may be either a thermostat, doing its own sensing, or a remote unit served by a detector or detectors.

System Loops

There are two types of simple control loop, namely 'open' and 'closed'.

The Open Loop System is when the movement of the controlled device has no effect upon the variable measured to initiate the control action, thus giving no feed-back and providing only general control. A typical example of an open loop is outdoor compensation whereby the external air temperature schedules the flow temperature through to the heating system via a controller and motorised mixing valve. The extent to which the required water temperature of a radiator system might vary with the outside air temperature is shown on the graph in Figure 4.6, the actual space temperature is only inferred.

The Closed Loop System is when the movement of the controlled device has a direct effect upon the variable measured, thus providing feedback and hence more accurate control. Thermostats linked to radiator valves or fan coil units are examples of such systems in which the actual space temperature is measured and controlled directly.

FIGURE 4.6: TYPICAL RELATIONSHIP BETWEEN WATER AND OUTSIDE TEMPERATURES

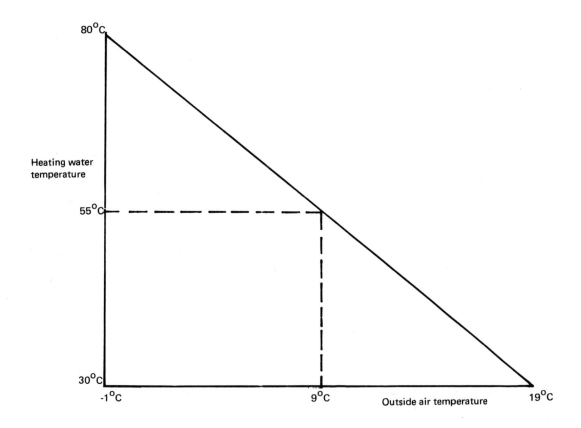

(The graph implies that inside air temperature should be around 19°C as a result of the interaction of the outside air and heating water temperatures as scheduled).

Combining system type with action type the following are representative applications:

Open Loop, Two Position: an air inlet control damper controlled by an outside air thermostat.

Open Loop, Proportional: a three port mixing valve controlled by an outside compensator (proportional controller) served by outside air and mixed flow water temperature detectors.

Closed Loop, Two Position: a circulating pump motor controlled by a room air thermostat.

Closed Loop, Proportional: a three port mixing valve controlled by a proportional controller served by a room air temperature detector.

These are shown in diagrammatic form in Figure 4.7.

System Power Sources

Generally controls are classified by the source of power operating them and there are four classifications:

Self-Contained: where the controller and controlled device are combined and operation is by either direct mechanical action or the expansion or contraction of a volatile substance caused by changes of the variable. A typical example is a thermostatic radiator valve.

Electric: where electricity is the source of energy and a signal is transmitted from the controller to power the controlled device; equally a signal may be transmitted from a detector to initiate the controller's transmission.

Electronic: again electricity is the energy source but the controller has an electronic amplifier to transform minute signal power initiated by changes in the variable up to a level which can power the controlled device.

Pneumatic: where compressed air is the source of energy for both signal transmission and powering controlled devices, the pressure employed is usually between 3 and 20 psig.

The manufacturer or qualified installer will recommend the appropriate power source and system for individual applications be they heating and ventilating, process usage or the handling and storage of hazardous materials.

System Lags

Allowing for system lags must be an important aspect of the initial control system design. In an air conditioning or ventilating system, for example, *distance and velocity lags* are incurred along the length of the pipework from the boiler to the heat exchanger and through the ductwork to the point to be heated. The air then has to travel across the room or space to be heated where a detector in the extract will pick up the sensed temperature.

In addition to these velocity lags, which can be quite considerable, there are also the *transfer lags* to be taken into account. These arise at the boiler where the heat is transferred into the water and also at the heat exchanger where the heat is transferred to the ducted air. Finally it should not be forgotten that the heated air when eventually delivered must then be transferred to the personnel and fabric of the building.

FIGURE 4.7: CONTROL LOOP SYSTEMS

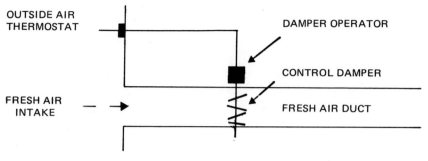

OPEN LOOP TWO POSITION

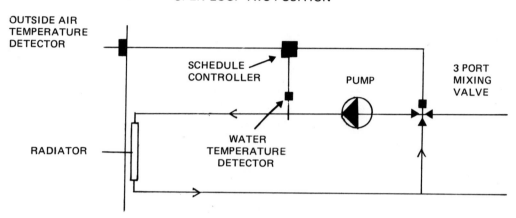

OPEN LOOP PROPORTIONAL

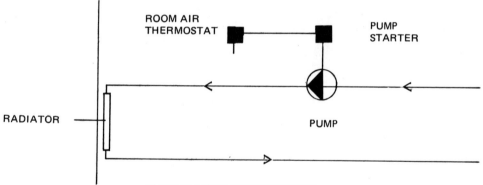

CLOSED LOOP TWO POSITION

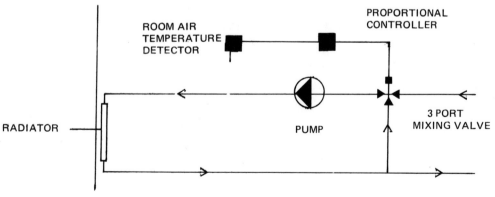

CLOSED LOOP PROPORTIONAL

Problems of Common Return

A problem frequently encountered with heating systems, resulting from careless pipework configuration, arises from a common return. This is illustrated in Figure 4.8. In this example there are two zones to be heated: the colder, north zone involving a water temperature of 64°C and the warmer, south zone which requires its water at 52°C.

The design allows for the supply of water to the south zone at the required temperature by mixing the flow direct from the boiler with that returning from south zone's radiators. But, as can be seen, the return water from the north zone was mixing with it thereby raising its temperature back to south zone to above 52°C. Diverting the return water from north zone to beyond the junction was therefore necessary before the supply temperature conditions to south zone could be achieved.

Control Economy

There are many measures that can be undertaken to improve control economy. Likewise there is a variety of equipment available from simple thermostats to sophisticated building management systems. This section concentrates on the simple, relatively low cost and routine measures that must not be overlooked. Discussion on new control equipment follows later.

Maintenance

Regular system maintenance is essential to keep heating plant and equipment at peak performance. Scaling, corrosion and material wear will inevitably take their toll over time bringing, at best, lower efficiencies and higher heating bills and, at worst, system breakdown. Members of the HEVAC Control Systems Group of Manufacturers offer preventative maintenance and further information can be obtained from the Association.

All the members of the HEVAC control manufacturers group offer control system service and some have expanded to cater also for the basic plant i.e. boilers, fans, refrigeration machines, etc., on a total maintenance basis.

Service contracts can be negotiated to suit virtually any client requirement in terms of number of annual visits, emergency call-out, replacement parts, expendable parts (lubricants etc).

A typical control service contract may involve annual contractual charges for four visits per year for cleaning, checking, adjustment etc., with additional charges for both replacements and breakdown emergency call-out visits as necessary.

If the client so requires, annual charges may be negotiated to cover all spares replacements and normal emergency call-out (12 hour maximum delay) whilst having separate extra charge-out rates for high priority (two hour maximum delay) call-out only.

On very large or complex installations it may be necessary to have a resident engineer, or even a team of engineers, permanently on the job site for the duration of the contract.

Economy Checklist

There are many control economy measures to be taken involving little or no financial expenditure but simply an understanding that these should be tackled and the knowledge to carry them out. They are listed in Table 4.9.

A simple measure to reduce energy consumption in heating and ventilating plant is to widen the proportional bands of the temperature points from the heating to the cooling application. This can be as wide as 10°F (6°C) with the heating not being activated above 65°F and the cooling cycle not taking over until 75°F. Throughout the 65-75°F range the valves remain closed ensuring that this 'dead band' gives maximum saving due to the action of damper modulation of fresh and recirculated air (see Figure 4.10).

FIGURE 4.8: PROBLEMS OF COMMON RETURN

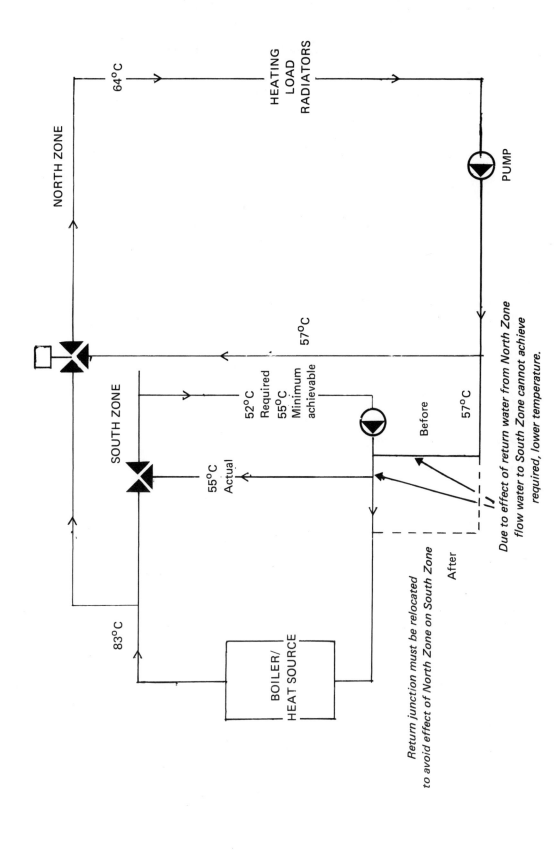

TABLE 4.9: CHECKLIST OF HEATING CONTROL ECONOMIES

1. Are the control points set in accordance with the overall system requirements?

2. Is the calibration correct?

3. Have tolerable limits been established within which the system can operate?

4. Have the sensors been correctly sited?

5. Is load or ambient reset used wherever possible to reduce energy consumption of outside compensation schedule controlled systems?

6. Is enthalpy control employed wherever possible instead of dry bulb temperature only control for free cooling applications?

7. Are plant operation costs minimised by the use of other methods and techniques such as optimum start control, load shedding, and the use of extended switching differentials and proportional bands?

FIGURE 4.10: THE PROPORTIONAL TEMPERATURE BAND

(Pneumatic Sequence Control)

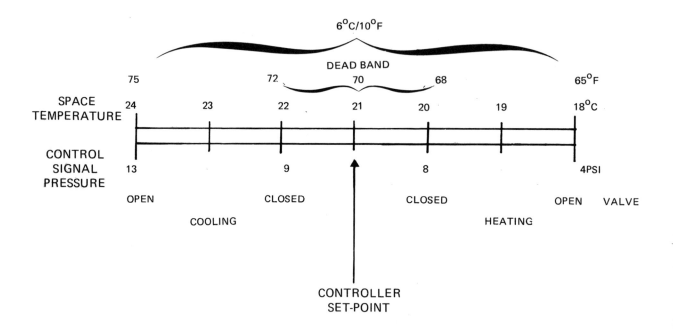

The correct positioning of internal and external temperature sensors is also important to the efficient running of heating systems. Internal sensors should be positioned approximately five feet (1.52 metres) from the floor. They should not be placed near windows, doors or radiators but at a point which reflects as accurately as possible the general room temperature. Similarly avoid chimneys, exhaust fans and windows and anywhere which may distort air temperatures when siting external sensors.

Point 5 in Table 4.9 relating to load and ambient reset means changing the set point of a flow controller in accordance with process or outside conditions to provide the correct flow temperature for the heating requirement.

An example of how ambient and load reset can be applied to existing controls is with the operation of refrigeration machines and water chillers. As Figure 4.11 shows, machine efficiency can be improved significantly for the same duty if the leaving chilled water temperature is raised and the leaving condenser water temperature lowered.

Clearly, the leaving chilled water temperature could be scheduled in accordance with the load on the system as determined by either the return water temperature or the positioning of the valves within the system. The condenser water temperature could be varied in accordance with the outdoor air wet-bulb temperature.

Psychrometrics

Point 6 of the checklist in Table 4.9 referred to enthalpy control in preference to dry bulb temperature only control. This takes the discussion forward to embrace relative humidity and the enthalpy, or total heat, of the air including its water content.

An understanding of psychrometrics, which could also be called the study of air conditions, is of fundamental importance in the design of air-conditioning systems and humidified warm air systems and their attendant controls arrangements.

Air has the ability to hold varying amounts of water vapour in suspension dependent upon its temperature and barometric conditions in accordance with Dalton's Law of partial pressures.

The easiest way to appreciate and work with psychrometrics is by use of the Psychrometric Chart. An example is given in Figure 4.12. For any given air condition, internal or external, the psychrometric chart shows the relationship between:-

—dry bulb or sensible temperature
—wet bulb or ultimate adiabatic saturation temperature
—relative humidity or percentage saturation
—specific moisture content and its corresponding dew point (saturation) temperature
—specific enthalpy (total heat) content of the air/moisture mixture.

If any two of the above five factors are known then the other three may be obtained from the chart. So it can be seen from the figure that armed with readings of say the dry and wet bulb temperatures it is a straightforward exercise to read off the moisture content, dew point and enthalpy. From this basis, the mixing of air at two different conditions may be plotted and the resultant heating, cooling, humidification, dehumidification etc., loads be calculated.

Enthalpy Switchover

One energy conservation implication from psychrometrics is the technique of enthalpy based economy switchover. In most air conditioning systems, there is usually scope to employ 'free cooling', that means satisfaction of internal cooling requirements by the introduction of outside air alone, without having to switch on refrigeration plant.

In such cases, when there is control provision to vary the amounts of fresh air and recirculated air, 100 per cent fresh air would be employed and as the internal cooling load increases the refrigeration plant would be sequenced into operation. But, simultaneously, the outside air

FIGURE 4.11: CHILLER OPTIMISATION

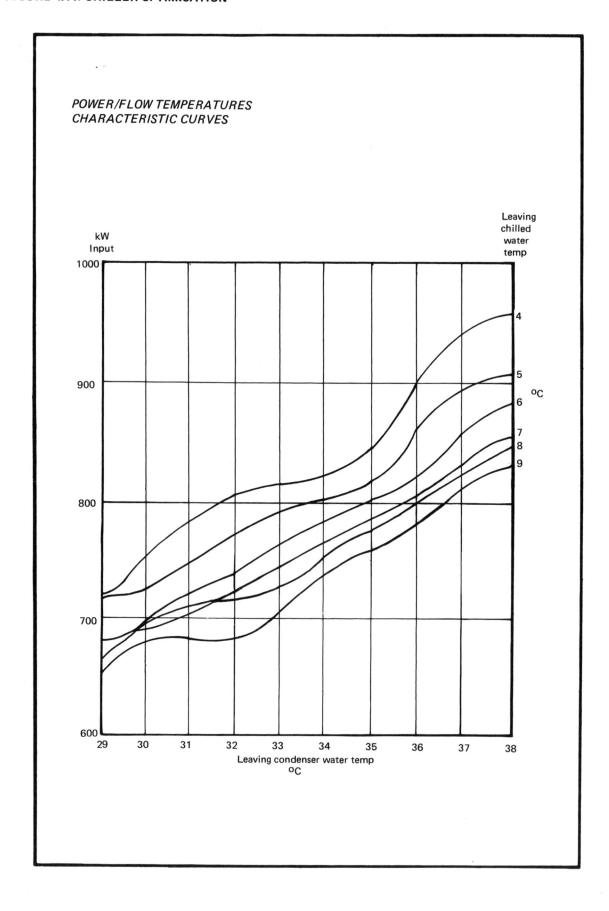

FIGURE 4.12: THE PSYCHROMETRIC CHART

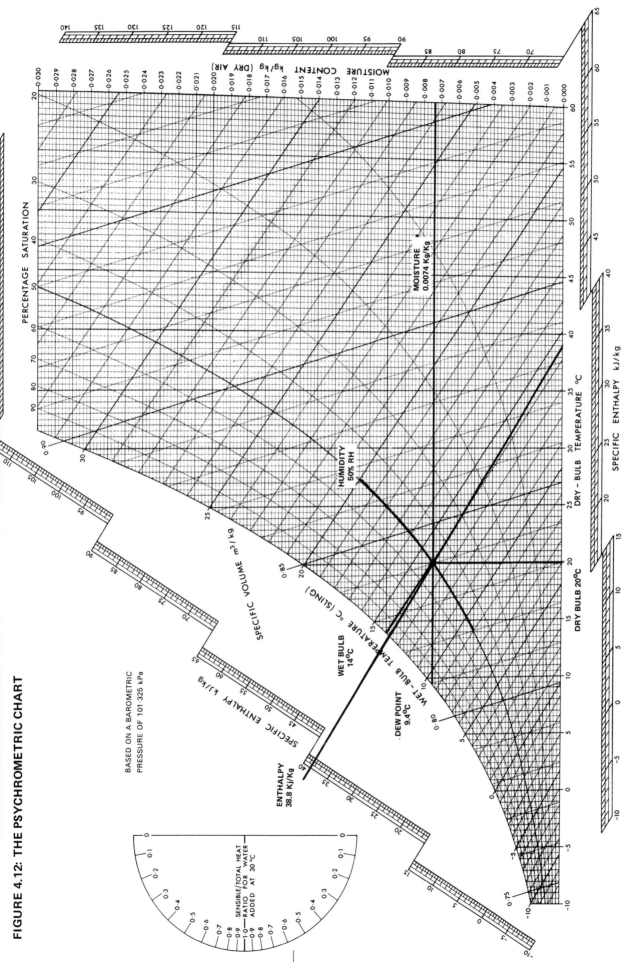

Source: *Psychrometric Charts reproduced by permission of the Chartered Institution of Building Services*

temperature and humidity may also be increasing and thus, to maintain minimum load on the refrigeration plant, there comes a point when it is more energy effective to revert to minimum fresh air and maximum recirculation.

For many years this 'economy switchover' was achieved by an override thermostat with a set-point some 2 to 4°C below inside dry bulb set-point temperature which effected the necessary damper action. However, this technique only involved implicit assumptions about fresh and recirculated air humidities and thus could be uneconomic in non-average conditions.

Enthalpy based switchover, as the name implies, takes account of the total heat in both the fresh and recirculated air streams and switchover to maximum recirculation will occur when the fresh air enthalpy rises above the diagonal line in Figure 4.13 indicating the recirculation (space) condition and the reverse when the fresh air condition falls below the line.

In the case of dry bulb switchover, were this based upon a set-point of say 18°C for space set-points of 20°C and 50 per cent RH, relative humidities in excess of 70 per cent at a dry bulb temperature of 17°C would result in uneconomic loading of the refrigeration plant, just as would relative humidities below 40 per cent at a fresh air dry bulb temperature of 22°C.

Time and Optimum Start Control

Time controls on heating plant are probably the most important items of energy-saving equipment.

Time control is clearly on/off, or two position in these defined terms, and as such is the initiator of the operation of control systems as well as boilers, pumps, fans, etc. More importantly time control also stops the operation of equipment much more effectively than by manual means.

The equipment varies from the simple time switch through to the latest optimal start programmers which combine time and temperature measurements to delay plant start-up to the latest time compatible with building occupancy requirements.

In the ideal case the space temperature within a building should be capable of being raised instantly at occupation time to the required level and then again reduced instantly at the end of the day. Obviously this cannot be achieved in practice as there has to be some heating up time and cooling down time before and after the occupancy period.

With fixed time start, the variation in outside temperature will affect the length of the heating up period required: the required temperature being reached more quickly in mild weather. And if the start time is selected for an average outside temperature then, again, during severe weather there will be underheating during the early period of occupancy.

Variable time start is clearly an advantage and this is achieved, see Figure 4.14, by sensing the internal and external temperatures. With plant and building responses built as parameters into the controller the heating plant can then be activated at the latest point possible to provide the required temperature on occupancy.

Optimum start controllers are now in widescale use in industry and commerce and there are many examples of substantial energy savings and short payback periods being achieved.

The full cost of an £800 system was regained in a year at a telephone exchange with basement and three floors. The volume of the building was 150,000 cubic feet (4,250 cubic metres) and the boiler capacity 720,000 Btu's per hour.

Fuel savings in excess of £1,000 per year also gave a payback inside twelve months from an optimum start control system at a group switching centre. This building comprised a basement and six floors, with a volume of 900,000 cubic feet (22,650 cubic metres) and a boiler capacity of 3.1 million Btu's per hour.

Building Automation Systems

These fast developing systems find particular application in larger, more complex buildings which require the application of more sophisticated equipment to achieve maximum operational benefit in building services.

FIGURE 4.13: ENTHALPY SWITCHOVER

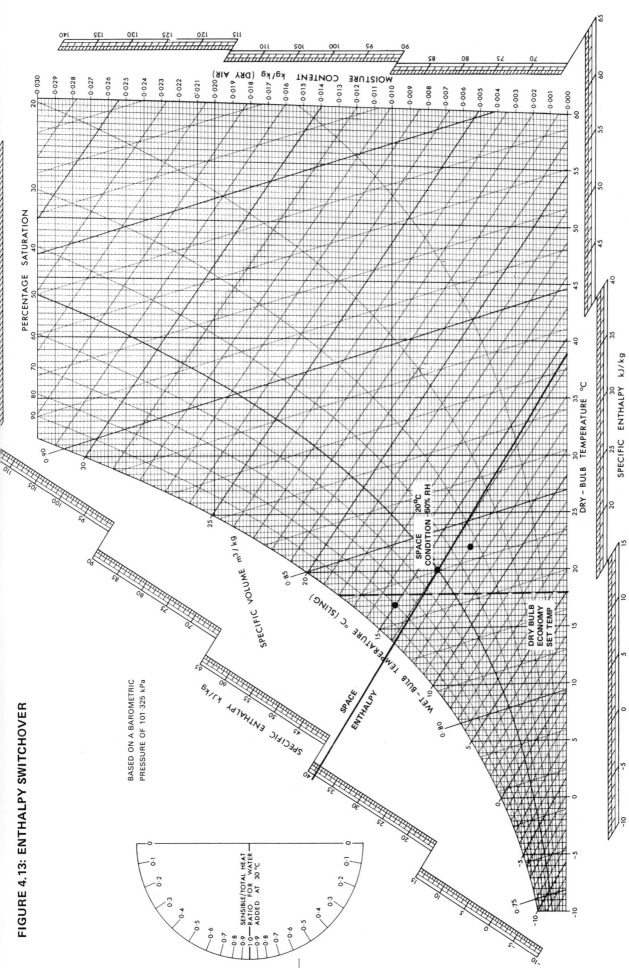

Source: Psychrometric Charts reproduced by permission of the Chartered Institution of Building Services

The systems are normally made up of six elements:

 –the field interface devices, the sensors, relays etc
 –field processing units to accept the information and initiate the action
 –two wire or co-axial cable loop connecting these remote panels
 –the central processor
 –the operator's console to input information into and to access data from the system
 –peripheral equipment such as printers, annunciators, graphics etc.

System Functions

In essence a building automation system will perform all building management functions: the start and stop control of plant; status reporting; control point adjustment; audio monitoring; analogue indication; alarm annunciation; data logging; start/stop programming; graphic displays and totalisation of data.

But the system will, in addition, carry out a series of complex energy management programmes as listed in Table 4.15.

Firstly there is the facility for ambient reset, i.e. the continuous resetting of an outside compensation schedule or ambient reset. The schedule dictates the basic air or water flow temperature in accordance with outside air temperature and the reset action modifies the schedule in accordance with actual inside air temperature. Multichannel application of optimal start programming ensures that individual zones achieve their required conditions with the minimum pre-heating or pre-cooling period independently of each other. The multipoint sensing of flow rates, temperature differentials and operating times offer computerised integration to indicate energy consumption, plant efficiency, operating costs etc.

As stated in Point 4 of the table, the reduction of heavy equipment starts is to avoid excessive maximum demand and/or electrical plant and equipment overload due to higher starting currents. The aim of maximum demand control is to take plant out of service at peak demand times and achieve a flatter load/time pattern. Load cycling, or duty cycling, is particularly effective in achieving savings in both fan motor electrical consumption and demand costs and fresh air heating energy consumption costs.

Enthalpy control has already been discussed. The standard programme provides for optimal switch over from 100 per cent fresh air to maximum recirculation to minimise refrigeration plant loading. Lighting load reduction is undertaken by photo electric sensing and time control to maximise benefits from natural daylight in accordance with occupants' needs.

Boilers have very similar standing losses, due to combustion, shell heat radiation, blow-down etc., at 10 per cent firing rate as at 100 per cent firing rate. Thus it is preferable to have one boiler on line at 90 per cent rather than two boilers on line at 45 per cent load.

The greatest chiller efficiency is obtained when the difference between its chilled water and condenser water temperatures is at the practical minimum. The real-time computer programme involves sensing and integrating all flow and return water temperatures along with outside wet bulb temperature and then controlling the operation of the chiller and its attendant cooling tower.

Point 10 refers to the restitution of mains power after a failure. The various plant items are re-started in sequence to avoid coincidence of high maximum demands and starting currents. This final item is really an extension of Point 3 in the table as it initiates triggers for planned maintenance action and alarms in breakdown situations.

Other Aspects for Consideration

Good systems will also incorporate an English language prompt mode of operation to assist the inexperienced operator.

There are systems available today for virtually every type, size and mix of buildings with varying ranges of programme capability, point capacity and central station/outstation communication/ operation facility. Client choice will ultimately depend upon a balance of immediate needs, future expansion plans, management emphasis and projections of cost-effectiveness. But some factors to keep in mind are:

FIGURE 4.14: THE OPTIMUM START CONTROLLER

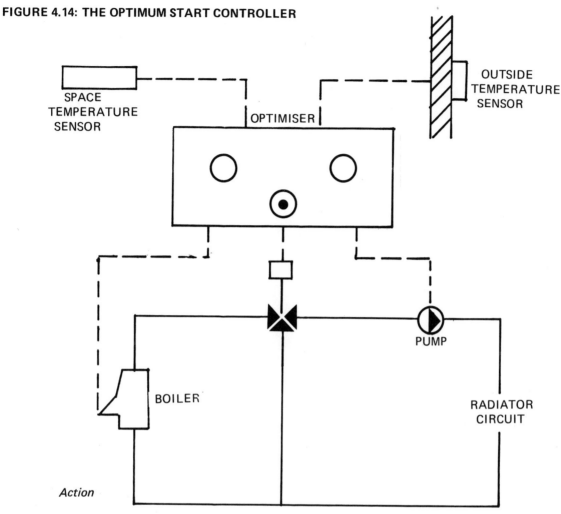

Action

1. *Starts boiler.*
2. *Cycles heating valve wide open until required inside temperature is achieved.*
3. *Starts pump.*

TABLE 4.15: STANDARD PROGRAMMES IN A CENTRALISED BUILDING AUTOMATION SYSTEM

1. Automatic load resetting of air and water systems.

2. Optimum start programmes for multiple plant.

3. Analogue, run-time and energy totalisation of plant components, systems and buildings.

4. Programmed start/stop including facilities for the reduction of high start frequencies for heavy equipment and the scheduling of all plant operations and holidays.

5. Maximum demand control, load shedding, load cycling and load processing to achieve minimum energy costs.

6. Enthalpy control of all applicable plants.

7. Optical and timed automatic lighting control.

8. Boiler optimisation with variation of parameters and sequence of the boiler plant.

9. Chiller optimisation.

10. Automatic load restarting on power failure.

11. Maintenance management of the system to keep plant at optimum efficiency either by run times or condition monitoring.

Size and location: equipment sizes vary from one manufacturer to another. One system, for example, comprises:

- a central processor unit (CPU) housed under a large desk with keyboard, VDU, and printer located on the top surface

- a distributed processor (DPU) handling up to 500 points

- a field processing unit (FPU) up to 16 points, with

- a field equipment unit (FEU) controlling relays, etc.

Central and distributed processors should be generally mounted in clean areas, with FPU's and FEU's in plant rooms or local to equipment to minimise hard wiring. Multiple VDU's and printers may be provided which can be mounted locally to, or remotely from, CPU's and DPU's.

Access and Security: access to the system is by password and may be limited to specific sections of data and software as required by clients. Heating and ventilating aspects can be reported/programmed in the engineers office and fire/safety/security aspects in the security lodge using separately addressed VDU's, printers, etc. Different levels of access clearance can be assigned to the various grades of staff involved, ranging from basic interrogation of the system, through parameter adjustment and up to complete programme editing.

Installation and Plant Operation: the main computer trunk is a twisted screened pair, very easy to install, and generally production need not be interrupted although weekend working or special shut-down arrangements would be necessary for final interface wiring and system testing and commissioning.

Case Study of a Building Management System

The study relates to the system's installation into a single, large factory building involved in light electrical engineering and electronics manufacturing.

A five day, single shift operating regime was in operation with the main boiler house kept on stream to maintain steam distribution mains up to temperature for as long as the external dry bulb temperature was below 15°C.

The manufacturing areas were physically divided into a series of bays, all with steam heating but varying in lighting and ventilation arrangements. The office areas were located along one side of the manufacturing bays.

The system was designed to improve energy efficiency in all fuel using areas, both for process and space heating.

SOLDER BATHS

The extraction systems were electrically interlocked with their respective solder baths, such that the baths could not operate without effective extract ventilation. However fumes were only generated when the solder surface was disturbed during manufacturing operations. During warm-up and non-productive times the fume problem did not arise.

Existing Operation

Manual Start/Stop Control

Total Motor Running Load	6.3 kW
Average Air Heating Load	39 kW
Running Time	Shift time, including ¾ hour lunch break, plus 2½ hours solder bath fixed preheat period
Operating Year	Fan Motors 48 weeks
	Air Heating 35 weeks

Proposals for Energy-Saving

Switch-off systems during lunch break and preheat periods.

Time Saving	3¼ hours per day; 5 days per week
Electrical Energy Saving	4,900 kWh per annum
Heating Energy Saving	22,200 kWh per annum
Electrical Cost Saving	£120 per annum
Heating Cost Saving	£265 per annum
Total	£385 per annum

LIGHTING CONTROL

Six of the manufacturing bays had high level general lighting in combination with low level task lighting local to operatives.

The task lighting was under manual control and the general lighting had retro-fitted time and photo-electric cell load control.

Existing Operation

Shift time control with photo-electric cell load modulation.

Installed Load	175 kW
Average Load Diversity	0.5
Average Controllable Load	87.5 kW
Operating Year	48 weeks

Proposals for Energy-Saving

Switch-off high level lighting during lunch break.

Time Saving	¾ hour per day; 5 days per week
Electrical Energy Saving	15,800 kWh per annum
Electrical Cost Saving	£395 per annum

MAXIMUM DEMAND CONTROL OF FORK LIFT BATTERY CHARGING

Even though savings could have been achieved by battery charging during off-peak times, the existing and required regimes were based on single shift operation. The effect was a reduction in maximum demand charges, but by load/time programming rather than by dynamic load shedding.

Existing Operation

Individual, manual start/stop of 80 charging units during normal shift time.

Total Average Charging Demand	192 kVa
Average Charging Time	7½ hours

Proposals for Energy-Saving

Establish four equal demand groups of chargers and spread operational time over ten hours with only three groups on-line at any time to reduce peak maximum demand.

Demand Saving	48 kVa
Cost Saving	£960 per annum

DUTY CYCLING

Only one manufacturing bay had a supply ventilation system of any significance and this was arranged for variable off time (VOT) duty cycling in accordance with inside temperature and humidity limits. The 25 per cent rate is in fact the anticipated average cycle-off time which will range in practice from about five per cent according to condition variations up to a prescribed maximum of 50 per cent.

The cycle-off rate is set against 30 minutes overall periods to coincide with electricity demand charging periods to maximise the cost saving benefits of cycling the fan motor.

Existing Operation

Fixed time-clock start and stop control

Motor Running Load	12 kW
Motor Maximum Demand	14 kVa
Average Fresh Air Heating Load	160 kW
Running Time	9 hours per day
Operating Year: Motor	48 weeks
Air Heating	35 weeks

Proposals for Energy-Saving

Operate a 25 per cent rate of duty cycle-off time programme i.e. 7½ minutes off in each 30 minutes.

Time Saving	2¼ hours per day; 5 days per week
Electrical Energy Saving	6,480 kWh per annum
Electrical Demand Saving	3.5 kVa
Heating Energy Saving	63,000 kWh per annum
Electrical Cost Saving, Units	£160 per annum
Demand	£ 70 per annum
Heating Cost Saving	£760 per annum
Total Cost Saving	£990 per annum

HEATING TIME AND TEMPERATURE

The continual availability of steam throughout the heating season made wastage a very easy status quo to maintain under the guise of ensuring comfort conditions in the office block.

For this reason the savings are very large compared to what they would have been from applying optimum start and stop control only to an already set-back controlled system (a common occurrence in practice).

Existing Operation

Pump Motor Running Load	1.8 kW
Average Heating Load	235 kW
Weekly Occupied Times	42.5 hours per week
Operating Year	35 weeks

Proposals for Energy-Saving

Operate normally during occupied times with optimal start and stop and with low limit operation at other times.

Average Time Saving,	Pump Motor	18 hours per week
	Heating	18 hours per week at average load
	Plus 100 hours per week at two-thirds average load	
Electrical Energy Saving		1,130 kWh per annum
Heating Energy Saving		698,000 kWh per annum
Electrical Cost Saving		£ 30 per annum
Heating Cost Saving		£8,370 per annum
Total Cost Saving		£8,400 per annum

OPTIMAL START/STOP

Very substantial savings were to be had from the straightforward introduction of optimal start/stop to the general steam heating and primary systems.

Existing Operation

Fixed time-clock start and stop of steam availability to individual heating systems with frost protection override.

Average Heating Load	4,050 kW
Fixed Preheating Start Time	2½ hours before shift start
Fixed Heating Stop Time	Shift Finish
Operating Year	35 weeks

Proposals for Energy-Saving

Operate optimal start and stop of steam availability in accordance with variances of outside and inside conditions.

Average Time Savings,	Optimal Start	1 hour per day;	5 days per week
	Optimal Stop	¾ hour per day;	5 days per week
Heating Energy Saving		1,240,000 kWh per annum	
Heating Cost Saving		£14,900 per annum	

COSTS AND BENEFITS

Equipment for the system was costed at £56,000 which, with £9,000 allowed for associated builders work, pipework and wiring modifications, brought a total cost of £65,000. Table 4.16 shows how these costs break down within the six areas discussed above and compares these with the energy-saving achieved.

These figures show a basic pay-back period of approximately 2½ years and, in this case, high-light the major savings to be achieved from optimal start/stop and through limiting time and temperature. The savings quoted in this example are, of course, specific to the individual require-ments of that case. They should not be taken as a generalisation as in other cases different features may well appear as the most cost effective according to local conditions and requirements.

In some respects energy conservation installations are executed in industry for the wrong reasons and tend to diminish their true immediate cost-effectiveness. The great majority of engineering managers want management systems to improve monitoring and operation. The energy manage-ment banner allows them to show immediate savings and thus finance an initial monitoring/ management system capability which, once the system is installed, may be expanded in the future to serve both energy and operational management needs at much improved cost-effectiveness.

Conclusions

In summing up we can identify four areas of key importance in ensuring heating controls are being employed to maximum advantage. **Maintenance**—is all equipment working and functioning correctly as intended? **Regulation**—are distribution systems for air, water, steam etc. properly balanced to suit load requirements? **Control**—are set points those required for the operation and are the controls properly calibrated (control maintenance) to achieve the set points? **Computerised Energy Management**—what can now be done to further eradicate human error and to compensate for the maximum amount of variables which effect operational requirements? Furthermore, what can be done to monitor the trends and effects of the previous stages? Controls cannot control the un-controllable, but they will minimise the costs of operating well maintained, load matched capacity, services system. Computerised management systems may appear expensive at first, but once the central equipment has been installed, future field point extensions may be added at marginal costs only and experience has shown that system operators can achieve savings far in excess of original projections.

TABLE 4.16: SAVINGS AND COSTS ANALYSIS

Feature	Cost £	Saving £ per annum
Central Processor & I/O Devices	45,000	—
Field Equipment & Installation		
1. Optimal Start/Stop	7,640	14,900
2. Heating Time and Temperature	1,820	8,400
3. Duty Cycle	1,450	990
4. Maximum Demand	3,270	960
5. Lighting	2,180	395
6. Extract Ventilation	3,640	385
	£65,000	£26,030

5

INSULATION

Alan Williams

This chapter is intended to help energy managers ask the right questions about insulation and either answer these questions or indicate where answers might be sought.

Insulation is rarely a simple matter of retaining heat or maintaining low temperatures. It must cope with moisture vapour, access for maintenance, ventilation, acoustic problems and many other aspects of plant/building performance. Any requirement for insulation must clearly take account of these aspects and they should not be forgotten in the thermal considerations which dominate what follows.

Few topics are as central to energy managers as insulation and few topics as neglected nationally, industrially and domestically. The Select Committee on Energy in its 1982 report pointed out that of 504 local authorities about 300 were not actively engaged in energy conservation programmes and that only 20 per cent of the existing building stock has been tackled. It has been estimated that at least nine million out of the UK's 20 million households have inadequate loft insulation and seven million have uninsulated cavity walls.

Insulation is a complex subject and the chapter which follows is necessarily little more than a broad picture of the relevant motivations, materials and methods. It is inevitable that some perfectly valid, cost effective materials etc will be omitted. A list of commercially available insulants would fill a library shelf.

Why Insulate?

Money

The primary incentive to insulate is to save money. The energy manager's performance is judged primarily on financial grounds, by the amount of money saved rather than more complex criteria like process efficiency or thermal performance. Insulation payback calculations are, or can be, more complicated than for other measures that the energy manager adopts. With insulation it is necessary to assess the appropriate economic thickness. This will differ depending upon assumptions about weather, building occupancy, process conditions, building lifetime etc.

Consider the apparently simple case of a steam pipe in the roof of a building:

—is it live all year?
—is the building heated all day?
—is the pipe before or after timer/valve controls?
—does it have bleed flow during summer?
—does it serve a heating system or process?
—is access easy?

The Department of Energy Fuel Efficiency Booklet No 8 gives a comprehensive method of calculating the economic thickness of insulation for hot pipes. The example in Table 5.1 underlines the dependence of the energy manager's case upon the answers to some of these questions.

These simple calculations—where payback is simply cost divided by annual savings—are the usual first step in the financial case study (see Chapter 3). In this example there can be little doubt that insulation is cost-effective.

TABLE 5.1: EXAMPLE COSTINGS FOR THE INSULATION OF STEAM PIPES

Given:

Steam temperature	150°C
Pipe diameter	50mm
Pipe length	100 metres
Steam cost	£0.34 per therm

Use preformed rigid fibrous sections:

Economic thickness of insulation	50mm
Installed cost of installation	£5 per metre
Total installation costs	£500

Four sets of alternative conditions:

(a) Pipe in external area
(b) Pipe in building requiring continuous heating
(c) Pipe in building heated 12 hours per day and without a timer
(d) Pipe in building heated 12 hours per day with timer installed.

Energy savings:

(a) 8,926 therms per annum: £3,034
(b) 4,657 therms per annum: £1,583
(c) 6,597 therms per annum: £2,243
(d) 2,426 therms per annum: £ 825

Simple paybacks:

(a) 2 months
(b) 4 months
(c) 3 months
(d) 7 months

Note: The cost of installation assumes that there is no other maintenance reason to create scaffolding access to pipes. If there is, then this cost and the payback period would be reduced.

Money is clearly the primary incentive to insulate but there are four others, process technology, environment, regulations and appearance.

Process Engineering

There may be demands for insulation to maintain the quality of a fluid stream. In the simple case of heavy fuel oil transport there could be no flow at all if feed pipes were unheated and/or un-insulated. Similarly cold water pipes, where exposed to the danger of frost, need insulating to an appropriate thickness defined by the Property Services Agency in the following table. It should be stressed that these thicknesses will not prevent frost damage in deep or extended periods of frost, especially when the water in the pipes is stagnant. All insulation simply delays heat transfer and therefore the spread of frost.

TABLE 5.2: THICKNESS OF INSULATION FOR COLD-WATER SERVICES—FROST PROTECTION

	Declared thermal conductivity (W/m°C)					
	Pipework within buildings			External pipework		
Size of tube	0 to 0.040	0.040 to 0.055	0.055 to 0.070	0 to 0.040	0.040 to 0.055	0.055 to 0.070
mm	Minimum thickness of insulation (mm)					
15	32	50	75	38	63	100
20	32	50	75	38	63	100
25	32	50	75	38	63	100
32	32	50	75	38	63	100
40	32	50	75	38	63	100
50	25	32	50	25	44	63
65	25	32	50	25	44	63
80	25	32	50	25	44	63
100	19	25	38	25	32	50
125	19	25	38	25	32	50
150	19	25	38	25	32	50
Flat surfaces	19	25	38	25	32	50

Source: The Property Services Agency. Engineering Specification. Standard Specification (M & E) No. 3.

Process technology demands can relate to chemical, physical or biological changes in the fluid flow which insulation may control and which will modify the simple criterion of cost of lost energy. The question will now be not whether to insulate but by how much in order to allow the process to continue. Extra pumping costs, alternative costs of larger pipe diameters will be added to the cost of lost energy if the pipe is not insulated.

Environment

The environment influences the need to insulate in three respects, comfort, safety and atmospheric conditions.

Comfort is a major influence in the decision, for example, to double-glaze a living room and it often overrides complex thermal loss/solar gain calculations. Comfort may require insulation for acoustic or vibration control.

Safety can influence insulation specifications for a wide range of reasons:

—if hot pipes are accessible to children in a school then they may need to be insulated to a greater thickness than is purely economic

—asbestos may need stripping and replacing or encapsulating regardless of cost

—fire protection is a very important and widespread need especially in industrial plant and can be provided by some insulant systems.

Atmospheric conditions may affect insulation levels or material choice if pollutants attack some pipe or cladding materials. In the simplest case a level of insulation, typically 15mm, may be needed on cold water pipes in heated areas to prevent unsightly condensation.

Regulations

The financial motivation to insulate may also be affected by the needs of regulations. Buildings, in particular, are subject to regulations governing insulation levels. These are usually related to a standard measurement of heat loss, the U-value (which is explained later). Regulations vary widely from country to country and the philosophy whereby regulations are defined also varies. Many countries, typically those in Scandinavia, issue regulations which force an improvement upon building performance. Others tend to follow what has become standard practice on simple financial grounds. This is the custom in the UK and it means that regulations here should always be regarded as the absolute minimum standard. There will, almost inevitably, be sound argument to improve on the regulatory standard.

Figure 5.3 shows mandatory thermal insulation standards for new housing: roofs; walls; and floors.

Appearance

Building design and planning requirements often dictate changes in specification of insulation. This is usually associated with making structures less obtrusive but insulated structures can sometimes be featured, such as the Pompidou centre in Paris or the new Lloyds building in London. It is a disturbing fact that apart from such prestigious examples the appearance is rarely a factor in the initial case for insulation but is often the overriding basis for judging the final installation. This paradox is discussed later in considering quality control.

The energy manager must assess the real reasons for insulating and so ensure that thermal criteria are put in a proper financial perspective.

What is Insulation?

In most cases buying insulation means buying air as this is the most effective common insulating medium. Insulation materials are simply designed to trap air in layers or in spaces within porous, cellular or fibrous materials. There are more sophisticated methods involving vacuum and low conductivity gases which are important in some special industrial/technical cases but these need not be discussed here.

It is assumed that some basic facts about heat are understood. If not and if progress is needed beyond the simplistic treatment which follows, then there are many guides to which reference can be made—and some of these are listed at the end of the chapter.

Insulation creates a resistance to heat flow (in precise analogy to electrical resistance to current flow). Thermal insulation can act in limiting the three forms of heat transfer: conduction, radiation and convection. In most practical cases the energy manager will be presented with problems in steady state and only those are considered here.

Insulation materials are normally understood as those limiting *conduction*: the clothes we wear; the refractory lining; the domestic cavity filling. Conduction of heat in a simple slab of material is characterised by being:

—proportional directly to the temperature difference across the material
—inversely proportional to the thickness of material
—directly proportional to the area of the material when measured at right angles to the direction of heat flow.

FIGURE 5.3: MANDATORY THERMAL INSULATION STANDARDS—NEW HOUSING

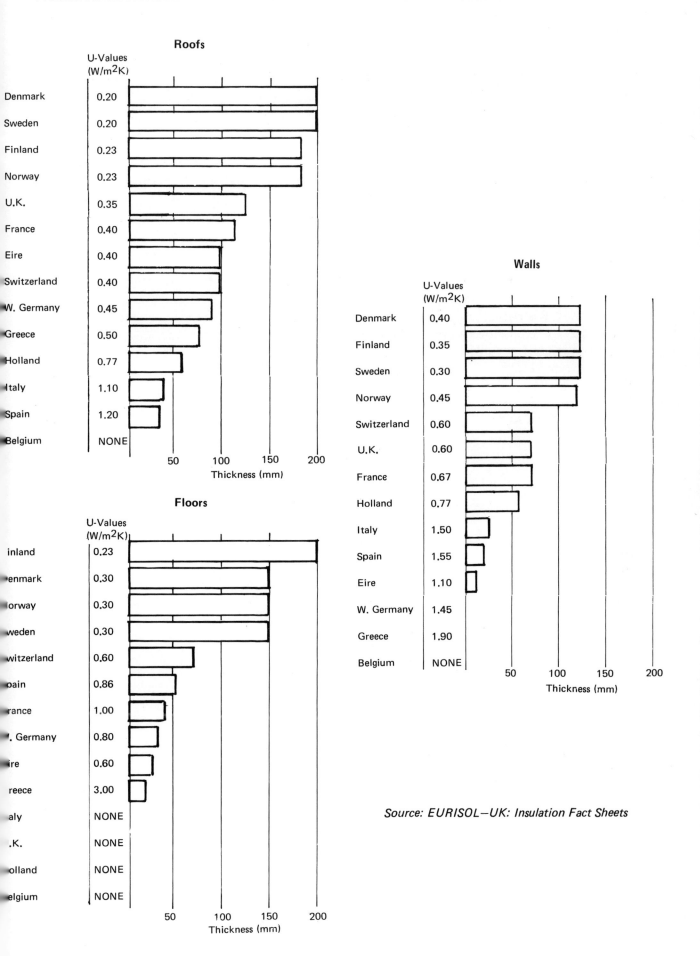

Source: EURISOL—UK: Insulation Fact Sheets

The quantity of heat flowing by conduction in unit time is Q where:

$$Q = \frac{KA}{L}(t_1 - t_2)$$

t_1 and t_2 are the two surface temperatures
L is the material thickness
A is the area of material, and
K is the constant of proportionality.

This constant is characteristic of the material and is called the *thermal conductivity* of the material. The more often quoted, and more useful, characteristic of the material is the *heat transfer coefficient* (or thermal conductance), h where:

$$h = \frac{K}{L} \text{ for a temperature difference of one degree}$$

But it is rarely the case that conduction in practice can be reduced to this basic simplicity which relates to a rectilinear block of uniform material with no heat flow restrictions at the material's boundaries. Restriction could be imposed by a fluid boundary layer or by scale built up in a boiler tube etc. The geometric factors for multilayer materials and for shapes other than rectilinear are a minor, if tedious, complication.
Some typical formulae are shown in Table 5.4.

TABLE 5.4: TYPICAL CONDUCTIVE HEAT TRANSFER FORMULAE

Simple Slab		$Q =$	$\dfrac{kA(t_1 - t_2)}{L}$
Composite Slabs		$Q =$	$hA(t_1 - t_2)$
	where	$\dfrac{1}{h} =$	$\dfrac{L_1}{K_1} + \dfrac{L_2}{K_2} + \ldots$
Simple Cylinder		$Q =$	$\dfrac{2.73\,LK(t_1 - t_2)}{Log_{10}\left(\dfrac{R_2}{R_1}\right)}$
	where	$R =$	Cylinder radius
Composite Cylinder		$Q =$	$\dfrac{2.73\,L(t_1 - t_2)}{\dfrac{Log_{10}\left(\dfrac{R_2}{R_1}\right)}{K_1} + \dfrac{Log_{10}\left(\dfrac{R_3\,t}{R_2}\right)}{K_2} + \ldots}$

Insulation to limit *convection* is not common. Hoods over elevated steam pipes are one, inefficient, example. Convection is, however, an important aspect of heat transfer and it affects insulation in many ways. Wind speed increases heat loss from exposed plant or buildings by convection because it removes the still air boundary layer which resists heat flow. Insulation in wall cavities is often more effective than expected because it eliminates convection losses in the cavity. As a rough practical guide if an air gap exceeds about an inch then convective heat transfer can be significant. This limits the gap between twin radiators and between radiators and the wall upon which they are mounted.
Convection is classified as *natural* or *forced*. *Natural convection* is due entirely to local temperature differences causing hot fluid, say air, to rise or cold air to fall because of density differences.

Forced convection is greater because fluid movements are supplemented by a fan, a pump or the wind. Convection is therefore characterised by the transfer of heat to or from fluids and the further conveyance of that heat to other surroundings. It is a complex phenomena and, by its nature, less precisely defined than conduction. Natural convection is often represented by an empirical equation of the form:

$$Q = C_1 (t_1 - t_2)^{1.25} L^{-0.25}$$

where Q is the heat transfer rate, $^\circ C$ cal/cm^2 S
   t_1 and t_2 are the surface and fluid temperatures $^\circ C$
   L is a characteristic dimension, centimetres
and C_1 has a value shown in Table 5.5.

There is a transition from conditions where there is smooth streamline flow of fluids to turbulence. Turbulence represents much greater heat transfer. This transition occurs at a value of Reynolds number of about 2,000.

Reynolds number $N_{Re} = \dfrac{VLp}{\mu}$

where V is the linear fluid velocity
   L is the characteristic dimension
   p is the density of the fluid
and μ is the dynamic viscosity of the fluid.

If N_{Re} is less than 2,000 there is streamline flow and little heat transfer. If N_{Re} exceeds 2,000 then there is turbulent flow and the fluid close to the surface of the solid is rapidly replaced giving greater heat transfer. In this case

$$Q = C_2 (t_1 - t_2)^{1.33}$$

TABLE 5.5: APPROPRIATE VALUES OF C_1 AND C_2 (in c.g.s. system)

	C_1			C_2		
Cylinders	8.9	x	10^{-5}	2.5	x	10^{-5}
Vertical Planes	1.03	x	10^{-4}	3.0	x	10^{-5}
Horizontal Planes Facing Up	1.0	x	10^{-4}	3.6	x	10^{-5}
Horizontal Planes Facing Down	4.4	x	10^{-5}	Irrelevant		

Source: Technical Data on Fuel: Ed Spiers 1962.

The complexities of forced convection put it beyond the scope of this chapter and reference should be made for further information to the textbooks listed in the references at the end of this chapter. For most insulation applications, however, it should be expected that forced convection will maintain the boundary surface temperature at or approaching that of the fluid. This will correspondingly maintain heat flow near the theoretical maximum.

The third form of heat transfer is *radiation* which is simply a function of the fourth power of the absolute temperature. All materials at all temperatures above absolute zero emit radiation and the practical concern is with the net radiation gain or loss.

$$Q = 6Ae\,(Ts^4 - To^4)$$

where A is the area

Ts is the absolute temperature of the material surface

To is the absolute temperature of the average ambient surroundings

6 is a constant, called the Stefan-Bolzmann constant ($=5.673.10^{-8}$ in SI units)

e is the emissivity of the surface

Emissivity is unity for a perfect emitter, called a black body, and less than unity for all practical insulation surfaces. Table 5.6 gives some typical emissivities.

TABLE 5.6: TYPICAL EMISSIVITIES

(Emissivity=Absorptivity)

Values as % of emissivity of black body, i.e. ideal absorber

		50°C	500°C	1000°C
Building bricks				45
Fireclay bricks				75
Silliminite				28
Silica				66
Magnesite				38
Natural concrete tiles				63
Painted surfaces all colours		94		
Aluminium paint		50		
Alumium	polished	4	6	
	rough plate	7		
	oxidised heavily	20	33	
Copper	polished	2		
	oxidised	60	88	
Steel	rolled sheet	56		
	rough plate	95	98	
	heavily oxidised	88	98	
	calorised	79	79	
Water	(0.1mm or thicker)	95		

Source: From data compiled by M Fishenden, Insulation Databook, Diamant Publications 1977.

Emissivity is the same as absorptivity. Good emitters are good absorbers. Emissivity varies with temperature and a value should be used in calculations which corresponds to a practical temperature. Table 5.6 highlights the difference between different forms of a material and different operational temperatures. For example the emissivity of polished aluminium at 50°C and that for oxidised aluminium at 500°C varies by a factor of 8.

Consider a practical case: heavy oil flowing in an insulated pipe. From the internal oil at temperature heat flows through, say, a turbulent layer to a metal pipe. Metal is a good conductor so it is the surrounding insulation which first resists the available heat flow. The metal cladding on the insulation, say aluminium, then transmits heat to its outer surface (conduction) whence it is radiated to the atmosphere. At the same time with an exposed pipe heat is lost by natural convection in still air and by forced convection if there is a wind.

The turbulence inside the oil maintains the temperature of the pipe at the oil temperature and the wind turbulence will maintain the outer skin of the insulation at ambient temperature assuming that the oil and wind are strong enough to destroy their boundary layers. Hence the rate control is likely to be the thermal resistance of the insulation. There are circumstances, however, in which each one of the stages described could be more important.

The relative importance of radiation and natural convection are typified in Figure 5.7.

In considering actual overall heat transfer in a complex situation like the example above it is sometimes convenient to use a single parameter to describe heat transfer. The U-value is the overall heat transfer defined in units of Watts/m² °C.

$$\frac{t_1 - t_o}{Q} = \frac{1}{U}$$

where t_1 is inside temperature
t_o is outside temperature
Q is total heat transfer.

U clearly depends upon radiation/convection to the hot face, conduction through layers to the cold face and convection/radiation to the cold space. Building regulations are usually framed in U-value terms.

U-values can be made more realistic by taking full account of the conditions at the point of use if these differ from quoted standard conditions. It is, for example, quite realistic to define an effective U-value for double glazing which is negative. In other words in a given building there is a net gain of useful heat through that window.

Consider again the example of a steam pipe in a building roof which serves a radiant panel. There is a temptation to consider the feed pipes to such panels as part of the radiant system and to leave them uninsulated. At best a convection hood is put over such pipes. Both waste a great deal of energy because 70 per cent of the heat loss will be lost upwards by convection and by radiation. It is also important to remember that if feed pipes to the panels are insulated then the quality of the heat supplied to the panels will be higher and the panels will operate more efficiently. A small difference in the temperature of a radiator makes a big difference when the fourth power law operates. Do not forget to ensure that the panels themselves are insulated on their upper surface.

Another practical example is the use of a reflective surface, say aluminium foil, on the wall behind radiators. Provided this is not mounted in such a way as to restrict the convective flow round the radiator it will, on an outside wall, prevent wasteful radiation to the wall and reduced radiator efficiency.

What to Insulate?

How does an energy manager decide whether a pipe, a roof or anything else needs insulating. There are often simple ways of establishing priorities. Consider a factory with a multitude of different roof types, various processes and types of building occupancy. Calculations for all situations would be complex and time consuming since various architectural constraints may confuse the treatment of each roof. A short-cut to all this effort might be to take an aerial infrared thermograph of the factory and mount a study on the roof which shows the greatest heat loss. If that case can be proved cost-effective then proceed to the next highest emitter and so on. If a thermograph is too expensive observe the speed of melting snow!

There are usually similar short-cuts to the more daunting problems presented to the Energy Manager. Insulating hot pipes is covered in the Department of Energy's Fuel Efficiency Booklet Number 8 which indicates the economic thickness. Remember that with the cost of energy escalating in future the price of fuel used should be higher than the current price by an amount dependent upon the life of the plant concerned. It is always more expensive to insulate twice in the lifetime of a plant or building than to put on a thicker layer from the start.

**FIGURE 5.7: CONVECTION AND RADIATION LOSSES FROM SURFACES IN STILL AIR
AT 70°F**

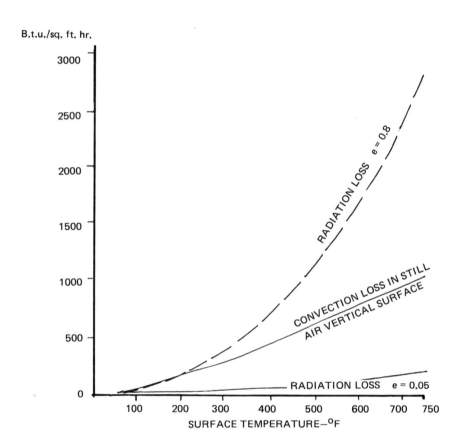

Source: The Efficient Use of Fuel, HMSO

The energy manager should begin with a clear idea of his reasons for insulating and set out his case for approval accordingly. If there are reasons difficult to cost, like comfort or appearance, then say so in order that all the motivations can be put in perspective.

The choice of what to insulate covers:

—the maintenance of cold or hot conditions
—vessels, pipes, ducts and chimneys
—plant above and below ground
—all types of buildings
—transport.

The procedure with all applications is the same: define the needs and cost the options.

How to Insulate?

Having decided that insulation is needed, for whatever reason, the energy manager must then review and cost the methods available to him to actually do the insulating.

There are two basic sets of choices:

—is the building/plant/pipe etc. to be insulated where it is manufactured or where it stands erected?

—is the unit to be insulated on the hot side or the cold side?

The first choice depends upon costs and the ability to protect the insulation through the erection process. It will usually only be done at the place of manufacture where standard or very large units are involved; standard because of economy of numbers and large, not usually because of economies of scale but, because additional on-site costs like scaffolding can thereby be eliminated.

In most energy management situations the first choice will be for the unit to be insulated where it stands erected.

The second option is more interesting. Take, for example, a kiln in which units are heated. There are insulating materials which can be fixed on the inside or the outside of the kiln. Both will save money. If the kiln is frequently cycled in temperature then less energy will probably be needed if the insulant is internal. This way the kiln walls will not be heated up as much and operational temperatures will be reached more quickly. If, on the other hand, the kiln is kept at temperature for a long time then external insulation will be preferred. The high thermal inertia of the kiln walls will then operate to advantage. The same argument also applies to some house designs in hot and cold climates.

It would be impossible to review all insulation methods for all situations. Figure 5.8 shows some methods for a limited number of applications. The series of insulation fact sheets published by EURISOL-UK are an excellent introduction to insulation methods for buildings. References at the end of the chapter cover industrial methods.

What to Use?

The properties of various insulants help to choose the material appropriate to each application.

Remember that you are buying air, in general, and the ability of the material to trap air is of prime interest. Thermal conductivity is simply a measure of this entrapment.

Mechanical strength can be important but should be judged when the material is installed with appropriate outer layer/s. Physical density is often quoted for insulants and given conductivity and appropriate mechanical strength then the lighter the material the better.

Thermal constraints may restrict the choice of materials and the energy manager should know maximum and minimum operational temperatures and also maximum/minimum temperatures under extremes of process and atmospheric conditions. The need for insulants to withstand thermal cycling, thermal shock, flexing, abrasion etc. will depend upon circumstances.

FIGURE 5.8: INSULATION METHODS: EXAMPLES FROM INDUSTRY

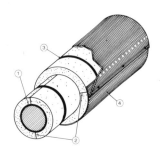

(a) Pre-formed pipe covering multiple layer construction

1. Pipe
2. Insulation
3. Securing wire or tapes
4. Jacketing with screws

(b) Flexible elastomeric pipe covering

1. Pipe   2. Insulation   3. Adhesive

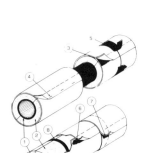

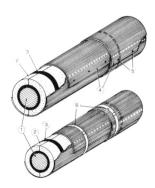

(c) Non-metal jacketing—field and factory applied

1. Pipe
2. Insulation
3. Adhesive or self-adhering lap
4. Staple-secured lap
5. Tape
6. Longitudinal overlap
7. Butt joint overlap
8. Securing wire or tape

(d) Metal jacketing—field applied

1. Pipe
2. Insulation
3. Securing wire or tape
4. Overlaps
5. Rivets or screws
6. Metal bands

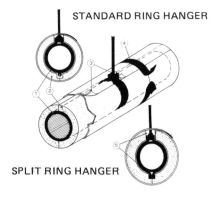

STANDARD RING HANGER

SPLIT RING HANGER

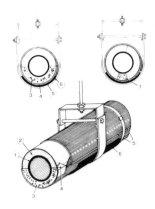

(e) Standard and split ring hangers

1. Pipe
2. Insulation
3. Overlap
4. Tape
5. Insulation adjusted to compensate for split ring hangers

(f) Clevis hanger—high density inserts

1. Pipe
2. Insulation
3. High density insulation insert
4. Vapour barrier jacket
5. Jacketing
6. Metal shield
7. Wood block insert

Figure 5.8: Insulation Methods: Examples from Industry (Cont)

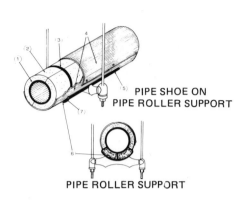

PIPE SHOE ON
PIPE ROLLER SUPPORT

PIPE ROLLER SUPPORT

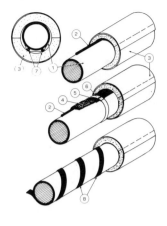

(g) Pipe shoe on roller support

1. Pipe
2. Insulation
3. Securing wire or tape
4. Jacketing
5. Pipe shoe (welded)
6. Insulation in shoe cavity
7. Pipe seal

(h) Piping—Traced

1. Pipe
2. Tubing tracer
3. Insulation with jacket
4. Heat transfer cement
5. Channel
6. Securing bands
7. Double tracer
8. Electric cable or tape tracer

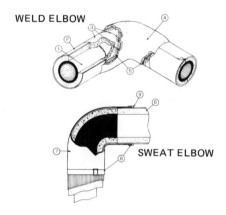

WELD ELBOW

SWEAT ELBOW

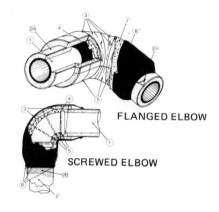

FLANGED ELBOW

SCREWED ELBOW

(i) Fittings—Elbow preformed

1. Pipe
2. Insulation with jacket
3. Securing wire
4. Vapour barrier mastic
5. Reinforcing cloth
6. Insulation
7. Preformed cover
8. Securing bends
9. Overlapping elbow cover

(j) Fittings—Mitred elbow

1. Pipe
2. Insulation with jacket
   A non metal
   B metal
3. Mitred covering
4. Glass fibre fill
5. Wire or banding
6. Elbow cover
7. Finishing cement
8. Cover fabric

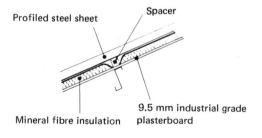

Profiled steel sheet

Spacer

Mineral fibre insulation

9.5 mm industrial grade
plasterboard

(k) Roofs—over purlin lining

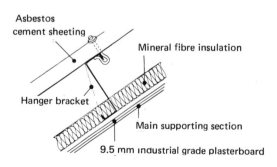

Asbestos
cement sheeting

Mineral fibre insulation

Hanger bracket

Main supporting section

9.5 mm industrial grade plasterboard

(l) Roofs—under purlin lining
    Separate lining board

Figure 5.8: Insulation Methods: Examples from Industry (Cont)

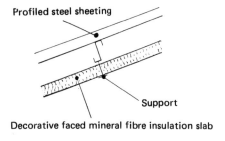

(m) Roofs—under purlin lining
     Decorative faced insulation slab

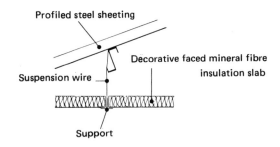

(n) Roofs—under purlin lining
     Horizontal suspended ceiling

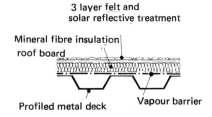

(o) Flat roofs—overdeck insulation

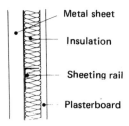

(p) Walls—lining inside sheeting rails

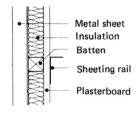

(q) Walls—lining outside sheeting rails

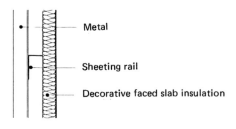

(r) Walls—decorative insulation slab inside sheeting
    rails

Sources: Examples (a)—(j) from the Mid West Insulators Contractors Association: examples (k)—(r) from
       EURISOL—UK.

Chemical resistance, fire resistance and protection against animal or fungal attack are also worth thinking about. Some materials, for example, make excellent nests! Another aspect which will likely emerge is the preferences and abilities of those available to do the job.

Table 5.9 gives a summary but energy managers should get the latest information on products which will always be improving.

TABLE 5.9: BASIC INSULATION TYPES

Rigid and semi-rigid insulation

Material	Form	Approximate Temperature Range ^{o}C	K cal/cm.s. deg C	Notes
Calcium -silicate (anhydrous)	Pipe Block	650 to 810	0.00013 at 95°C	Strong for weight. Good cutting. Water absorbent.
Foam glass	Pipe Block	Cryogenic to 320 possibly 650	0.00013	Strong. Water and vapour resistance. Weak abrasion resistance.
Glass Fibre	Pipe Board etc.	–40 to 460	0.000076 to 0.00015	Low conductivity. Many forms.
Other mineral fibre	Block Board etc.	120 to 1000	0.000086 to 0.00013	
Perlite foam	Pipe Block	to 810	0.00017 at 95°C	
Plastic Cellular	Pipe Sheets	–40 to 105	0.000086 & 0.000093	Elastomeric. Closed cells.
Polystyrene Foam			0.000069 &	Lightweight. Excellent cutting.
Phenolic Foam	Pipe Fittings	–40 to 80	0.000089	Combustible. Chemical composition continually developing.
Bead Board	Board			
Polyurethane	Pipe Fittings Board	–75 to 105	0.000055	
Refractory Fibre	Blanket Pipe Board	340 to 1250	0.00010 at 95°C	Used on high temperature surfaces.

Flexible sheets, rolls and blanket insulation

Material	Form	Approximate Temperature Range	K	Notes
Fibre glass	Blanket Roll	165 to 650	0.000076 & 0.00012 at 95°C	Many forms and facings.
Other mineral Fibre	Blanket Roll	450 to 540	0.000086	General purpose high temperature.
Refractory fibre	Blanket	340 to very high	0.000076 and higher	General purpose high temperature.

Note: Users should always check manufacturer's data sheets.

Source: Commercial & Industrial Insulation Standards. Mid-West Insulation Contractors Association.

Who Insulates?

Insulation, wherever it is utilised, needs to be installed with careful thought for its method of operation. Mis-application should be avoided by specification and design.

To give an example. If a building with a warm air heating system has a false roof installed which is so designed to allow, even encourage, warm air to flow above the false roof then it does not matter what the specified U-value of the false roof is. Temperatures above it and below it will be identical and its thermal properties are irrelevant.

Insulation in industrial and commercial situations can be undertaken by almost anyone. It is however invariably and demonstrably preferable to get the job done professionally. Even domestically contractors will not only carry out some insulation tasks more efficiently but because of practice, equipment and bulk purchase will do it more cheaply than the householder could.

Thermal insulation engineers (TIEs) working for a contracting company in TICA (the Thermal Insulation Contractors' Association) represent the safest way of ensuring a job efficiently done. Many of the larger companies will give some guidance as to what should be done. TICA will give advice about companies and deal with enquiries about companies installing marine, acoustic, cryogenic or any other kind of insulation. It publishes rates of pay for TIEs and controls this important aspect of industry. There are, in 1982, 169 member firms.

In the domestic sector there are again a number of firms which install insulation. It is always worth using a firm of repute, preferably of long-standing, so that you can expect them to outline and support their guarantees.

Quality Control

It is clearly illogical to invest in insulation and not obtain what was specified. There are four aspects of quality control which are frequently overlooked by energy managers. These are:

- —the consistency of the material used
- —the correctness of the installation
- —the performance of the installation, and
- —the maintenance of that performance.

Material should firstly be bought from a reputable manufacturer, direct or through a reputable supplier. The Thermal Insulation Manufacturers and Suppliers Association (TIMSA) will supply information. Their products will be closely specified and carefully packaged. It is worth remembering that insulation, once installed, is rarely seen again so that confidence in its initial quality is worth the expenditure of time and/or money.

Once supplied the material must be carefully stored before it is installed. If it is not to be installed by the company's own labour then time must be spent on supervision and a reputable contractor should be engaged.

There are many examples in industry where insulation standards are poor. Energy Managers have taken what appear to be bargains and got installations which may look good but in fact consist of cladding hiding inadequate thickness or quality of insulation.

Only when a plant is operational or a building occupied can the performance of insulation be verified. Verification may have to wait until the next cold spell or heat wave.

The verification stage is very rarely carried out by insulation users in any rigorous way. Perhaps the simplest method is to wait until the unit/building is at operational temperature, be it hot or cold. In the case of houses, commercial premises and warm processes the best time to monitor performance is on a cold dry day (or better still, night). View the installation through an infra-red imaging system. There are many such systems and a new generation of equipment developed for defence purposes is becoming commercially available. In a single scan the discontinuities in energy loss can be identified. With careful and practised interpretation these can be linked to particular faults or design elements. In the same way if a cold process is to be checked then a warm dry day (or preferably, night) should be chosen.

If infra-red systems are too costly to purchase remember that there are about five consultancies offering surveys using this type of equipment. If this is also too expensive then use surface temperature surveys. These should be accurately done using contact thermometers but, in the limit, use a sensitive hand!

The important thing is to check performance.

It is no use having spent all the time and effort discussed if insulation is allowed to get damaged and left un-repaired.

Figure 5.10 shows (from above) some pipe insulation at high level above an industrial access road. It has been used to facilitate access to valves and has clearly been damaged to the point where the pipe itself is bared. When viewed from below this insulation looked satisfactory. It should be maintained and protected from future 'unseen' damage by stronger cladding or independent access to the valves.

Figure 5.11 shows pipe insulation in the top of a heated building. The insulation has been applied carefully and to specification. Its performance and appearance are excellent. It is pointless carefully husbanding heat loss from pipes and the rest of the building heating system if the heat is allowed to escape through a big hole in the wall.

Continued maintenance of the insulation system can again be an in-house activity or it can be handed to a reputable contractor on a term contract.

Quality control and the maintenance of performance are neglected aspects of insulation usage. Even domestically few people check whether draughts have blown their loft insulation beads into a corner.

Having spent money on insulation it seems an elementary precaution to monitor and maintain its performance. Thermal performance should be measured before and after the insulation is applied to determine with acceptable accuracy the benefit gained.

Other Considerations

There are many aspects of process or building performance that impinge upon insulation. A few of these are noted briefly:

Asbestos

One authority which has not been mentioned although it has strong links with TICA is ARCA (The Asbestos Removal Contractors Association). In reviewing insulation materials the use of asbestos is now discouraged. Unfortunately many buildings and processes already have asbestos insulation and it is important that this is carefully maintained or eliminated. Health hazards from handling asbestos are appreciated and procedures are covered in Regulations and Acts of Parliament. The energy manager with asbestos insulation should consider its removal at the first opportunity. Advice on who can safely do this and reinsulate can be given by ARCA. The removal and safe disposal of the asbestos will then leave the energy manager with an installation which can be maintained, inspected and ultimately demolished more easily and cheaply. An intermediate option for the energy manager is to arrange for the asbestos to be encapsulated to limit health hazards. This simply postpones the ultimate removal problem.

Fire Protection

This is carried out either to impose a delay on the spread of flame or to protect structural members and processes long enough for fires to be extinguished. A wide variety of materials is

FIGURE 5.10: EXAMPLE OF DAMAGE TO HIGH LEVEL INSULATION

FIGURE 5.11: INSULATION RENDERED INEFFECTIVE BY POOR BUILDING MANAGEMENT

available commercially and the energy manager is advised to seek expert advice relevant to his particular problem (from specialist consultants or again from TICA).

Broadly speaking all non-flammable insulants will afford some measure of protection by retarding the heat flow from the source of the fire into the plant or structure. Special fire protection materials exist as cementitious fibrous sprays, boards or intumescent paints. This last group of products expands greatly at elevated temperatures and can be applied directly or supported on a substrate.

The ability of insulation to continue operating despite weather, water vapour, water or condensation attack is frequently necessary. Its failure to do so is often a cause of complaint against insulation. More often than not the fault lies in one or a combination of the following problems:

  —the misapplication of the right material
  —the poor maintenance of the right material
  —a misunderstanding of the laws of physics, or
  —the application of the wrong material.

Misapplication of the right material can result in failure: if moisture vapour barriers are pierced by fixing screws; if drain holes are omitted; if cladding is poorly jointed. This is a quality control problem.

Quality control is also at fault if the right material is not maintained. Water ingress can quickly diminish the insulating properties of an insulant. Water is used to promote heat transfer. The thermal conductivity of water at 100°C is twenty times that of dry mineral wool.

As for the laws of physics and their understanding consider a common domestic situation. In most rooms in a house water vapour will be created in addition to that present due to weather conditions. The creators are people who breathe out more water vapour than they breathe in, fires that convert hydrogen in their fuel to water vapour and cooking or washing activity which more obviously produces moisture vapour. If the house or room in question is progressively insulated and draught-proofed then that moisture production means that water vapour levels will increase. Water will then tend to condense on the coldest surface. This may be the window, or a spot on the ceiling above which loft insulation is missing, or water pipes. Wherever it is the cure is to dry the air by producing less moisture or by air conditioning or it is to control the ventilation. Insulation is frequently blamed—for doing its job!

If the wrong material is applied then problems could result from hygroscopic material or a deterioration of physical properties in the presence of moisture vapour. It is essential in the insulation of cold items to pay particular attention to the integrity of vapour barriers to avoid condensation and icing problems.

Mention has already been made of the regulations governing insulation. It is inevitable that such regulations will get more rigorous. This trend is worth considering in the design of a building or process. Even if a thickness of insulation which is 'ahead of its time' cannot be justified it is often easy to make sure that access exists to enable it to be fitted in later.

Another option for the energy manager is *shared cost* projects, briefly referred to earlier in the context of the first illustration.

A final example may serve to demonstrate this and some previous points.

In one particular factory building the energy manager studied his options for insulation. There were four:

  —do nothing (always an attractive option)

  —insulate the building. This was expensive because the roof could not support the extra weight and because scaffolding was expensive. Simple payback was in 10 to 15 years.

  —renovate the building structure

  —renovate the building and insulate.

Options 3 and 4 are simply analysed in Table 5.12. Any more sophisticated analysis would improve the strength of the conclusion.

TABLE 5.12: BUILDING 'X'. INSULATION COST CASE

	£
Original fuel cost (current prices)	40,000 p.a.
Fuel cost after insulation (current prices)	20,000 p.a.
Saving (current prices)	20,000 p.a.
Cost to renovate	90,000 p.a.
Cost to insulate at the same time (i.e. with shared costs)	60,000 p.a.

Option 3. Renovate without insulation

Year by year cost		Cumulative
Initial	£ 90,000	
Year 1	£ 40,000	£130,000
Year 2	£ 40,000	£170,000
Year 3	£ 40,000	£210,000

Option 4. Renovate and Insulate

Initial	£150,000	
Year 1	£ 20,000	£170,000
Year 2	£ 20,000	£190,000
Year 3	£ 20,000	£210,000

The Principal Trade Associations

TICA, Thermal Insulation Contractors Association, Kensway House, 388 High Road, Ilford, Essex IG1 1TL. Tel: 01-514 2120. Director: H Stroud. **ARCA, Asbestos Removal Contractors Association**, 24 Ormond Road, Richmond, Surrey TW1U 6TH. Tel: 01-948 4374. **TIMSA, Thermal Insulation Manufacturers & Suppliers Association**. Address as ARCA. Tel: 01-948 4151. **EURISOL-UK. Association of British Manufacturers of Mineral Insulating Fibres**, St Paul's House, Edison Road, Bromley, Kent BR2 0EP. Tel: 01-466 6719.

Useful References

Energy Conservation in Buildings, Fifth Report from the Select Committee on Energy, *HMSO 1982*. The Economic Thickness of Insulation for Hot Pipes, *Department of Energy Fuel Efficiency Booklet No.8*. Engineering Specification, Standard Specification (M&E) No.3, *Property Services Agency*. Insulation Fact Sheet Series, *EURISOL-UK*. Fuels and Fuel Technology, Francis, *Pergammon 1965*. The Efficient Use of Fuels, *HMSO*. Insulation Deskbook, *Diamant Heating and Ventilation Publications Ltd, 1977*. Thermal Insulation Handbook, Turner and Malloy, *Krieger Publishing Co Inc, 1982*. Commercial and Industrial Insulation Standards, *Midwest Insulation Contractors Association, 1979*. Technical Data on Fuel, Ed Spiers, *World Power Conference*.

6

COMBUSTION AND CONTROL OF PACKAGED BOILERS

Charles Hardy

The presence of excess air to the combustion process remains one of the main areas of energy waste in industry and commerce against which action can be taken at plant level. This chapter sets out the basic principles of boiler combustion and the techniques employed to obtain peak boiler efficiency. It also reviews the range of burners available on the market and factors affecting plant operation, such as pollution control.

As the largest number of boiler plants without any substantive form of combustion control exist in the shell boiler range from say 1,000 to 30,000 lbs steam per hour the chapter will concentrate on this type of equipment. The principles discussed will in many cases, however, apply to both larger and smaller plants.

It should also be noted at the outset that the chapter deals essentially with liquid and gaseous fuels and although the control of excess air to solid fuel plants is equally important combustion control devices for this fuel fall outside the scope of the chapter.

Principles of Combustion

Fuel consists in the main of hydrogen and carbon. Natural gas from the North Sea is mostly methane and with only a trace of other gases. Methane is one part carbon to four parts hydrogen. However heavy fuel oil has, apart from a goodly share of carbon, hydrogen and some sulphur along with other traces which are too small to warrant consideration in this context.

To burn these fuels the hydrogen, carbon or sulphur must be allowed access to oxygen. All that is necessary in practice to get the process going is to excite the fuel with a little heat, from an ignition source. Provided the fuel is divided into small enough particles combination will take place with the oxygen from the air giving rise to the generation of heat and the formation of new chemical compounds.

It is interesting to note that, as the oxygen is taken from the air, there is the recurring problem of the nitrogen which makes up 79.1 per cent of the total. This serves no useful purpose but rather enters the combustion system cold and leaves it hot with the increase in energy extracted from the fuel supply. It is a problem intrinsic to the design of modern industrial boiler plant which typically requires some degree of excess air.

If, however, a boiler plant is run with more excess air than is necessary then it can clearly be seen that not only is the nitrogen being heated which is left after the combustion process has mopped up the oxygen but excess oxygen and its related nitrogen are also being heated for no purpose.

Figure 6.1 illustrates the point in block diagram form. The rectangular cube on the left (Block A) represents a cubic unit of flue gas as it leaves the chimney in conditions of perfect, or stoichiometric, combustion of fuel oil. Block B highlights the problems of excess air.

Good combustion practice aims to get as close to Block A as possible. Unfortunately, however, for most plant operators equipment limitations as well as human failings combine more often than not to give conditions more closely aligned to Block B.

A word of warning must also be given about sulphur. If flue gases containing sulphur dioxide are cooled to a low temperature there is the risk of producing condensation in the chimney or

FIGURE 6.1: EXCESS AIR IN COMBUSTION

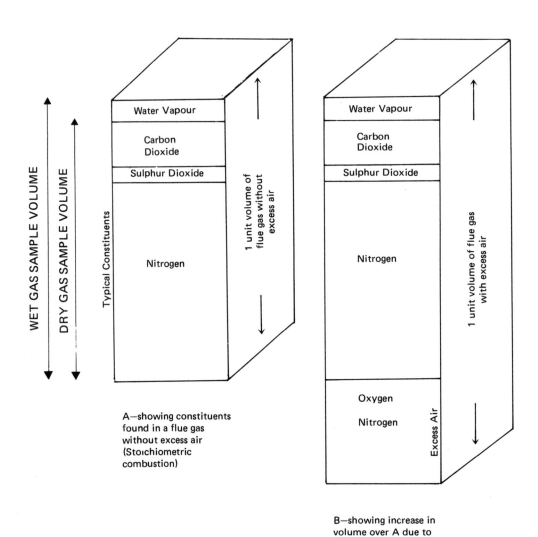

A—showing constituents
found in a flue gas
without excess air
(Stoichiometric
combustion)

B—showing increase in
volume over A due to
excess air

later stages of the boiler with the acid so formed attacking the metal parts of the plant. Natural gas, being devoid of sulphur, does not have this problem but care must be taken when using heavy fuel oil containing sulphur not to run a plant with flue gas temperature lower than say 350°F. The formation of corrosive sulphur compounds can take place if a burner is running with a large amount of excess air.

Avoiding Atmospheric Pollution

Before a method to control the ratio of fuel to air on any combustion process is established it is important to define accurately the operational factors which can affect the plant as a whole. The search for combustion efficiency must not be pressed to the detriment of other factors which may also affect performance.

The advent of atmospheric pollution control legislation has meant that it is an offence to emit from a chimney or flue more than a certain amount of solid matter into the atmosphere. This can be unburnt carbon, ash, scale or other solid matter that may have been generated during the combustion process or carried through the furnace from entrained matter in the combustion air or fuel.

On a national scale the largest source of solid matter chimney emission, excluding coal-fired plant, comes from the unburnt carbon loss from steam and hot water boilers firing heavy fuel oil. Gas-fired boilers should have no solid matter emission problems. If they do then there is the very likely danger of the production of large amounts of highly toxic carbon monoxide. Coal-fired plant has its problems in grit and fly ash emission but, as noted earlier, these lie outside the scope of this chapter.

The rate at which unburnt carbon is formed in heavy fuel oil-fired plant is dependent upon the following factors:

—the amount of combustion air excess

—the combustion chamber firing intensity

—the quality of atomisation of the fuel

—the quality of fuel/air mixing

—the amount of fuel compounds of the higher molecular weight category, broadly classified as asphaltenes, existing in the fuel

—the presence of elements in the fuel which act as combustion catalysts.

It can therefore be said that, in broad terms, the control of excess air to its minimum depends on how near the plant can be operated to the legal level of emission both from the solid matter emissions and smoke point of view. If, for instance, a boiler/burner combination could be designed for heavy oil firing to run at stoichiometric proportions, i.e. the exact amount of air for a given amount of fuel, then the boiler would be running at the minimum stack loss as far as excess air is concerned.

Understanding Plant Limitations

A combustion control system can only perform within the limits of the plant's capabilities and it is important for the operator that these should be known to him. The following series of illustrations (Figures 6.2—6.8) is given for guidance in this direction as an intending purchaser of an automatic combustion control system will need to discover his own plant performance criteria.

FIGURE 6.2: THE RELATIONSHIP BETWEEN EXCESS AIR AND STACK EMISSION

Cylindrical fire-tube boiler

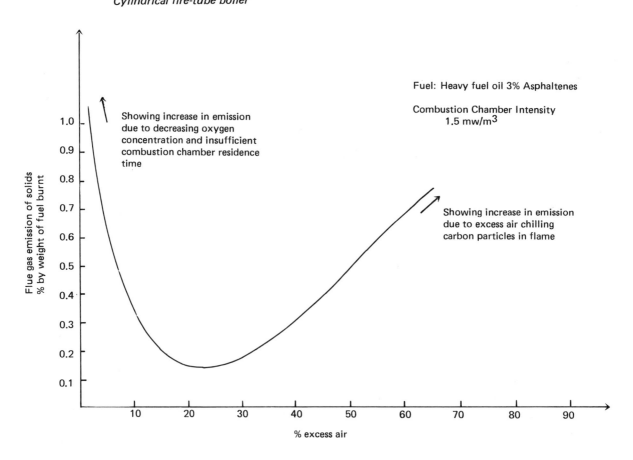

FIGURE 6.3: RELATIONSHIP BETWEEN COMBUSTION CHAMBER FIRING INTENSITY AND STACK EMISSION

Cylindrical Fire Tube Boiler

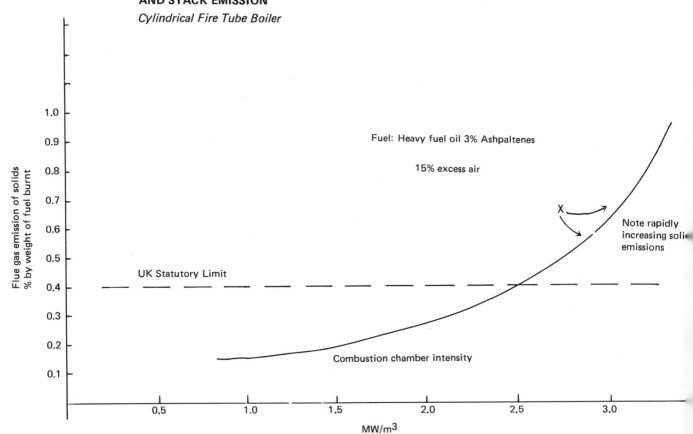

Excess Air

Figure 6.2 shows how solid emissions vary with excess air. A combustion controller fitted to this plant would be set, therefore, to control at say 3 per cent oxygen, i.e. 15 per cent excess air. Otherwise the boiler will start to emit high unburnt carbon levels. The limitation of the controller is therefore fixed by this important plant operational parameter. Information of this type should be sought by a prospective purchaser of new equipment. In the case of established plant discussions with the boiler or burner manufacturers may provide the necessary data.

Intensity of Firing

Figure 6.3 shows how the combustion chamber intensity of firing has an effect upon the emission of solid matter. (The interpretation of the previous graph must be made with this in mind). It can clearly be seen from Figure 6.3 that the operation of a boiler plant above 2.5Mw/m^3 of furnace heat release on heavy fuel oil is fraught with pollution hazard.

The rapid increase of emission level shown at the point X is due to the onset of carbon particle impingement on the furnace wall. This indicates that the particles are extinguished or quenched by this contact with a relatively cold surface. The re-entry of a chilled sponge-like sphere of coke, known as a cenosphere, back into the main flame gas stream does not give enough time for the particles to complete combustion. It therefore passes out of the furnace into the tube nest and to the stack as an unburnt particle. The graph illustrates, therefore, how important it is for the flame to be tailored to the combustion chamber so that it does not impinge upon the walls (a subject returned to later in this chapter).

Fuel Oil Viscosity

Figure 6.4 shows how atomisation is affected by the viscosity of the fuel oil. The objective must be to obtain the finest degree of atomisation possible within sensible economic bounds. The graph shows that a combustion control device will not be able to operate efficiently if the burner plant is not operated at the optimum viscosity.

Plant operators should know in advance from their fuel suppliers of any change in fuel oil viscosity, so that the atomisation temperature may be adjusted on the fuel oil heaters. A case can be made on very large plants for automatic control of viscosity, but careful investigation should be undertaken into payback time of the capital invested. The fact remains however, that modern research work has shown that stack solid emission levels can be effected by incorrect atomisation viscosities.

The design of the atomiser fitted to the boiler plant must certainly come under scrutiny: if it is worn, of a poor design, or just simply, as in so many cases, mechanically abused. If the first operation of the combustion process, atomisation, gets off to a bad start then combustion control cannot really be expected to be maintained at a high level. See Table 6.5.

Flame Shape

Figure 6.6 shows how the flame shape can be varied by the aerodynamics of the airflow through the burner. The illustration is included to highlight the importance of maintaining the 'as installed' dimensions of the equipment, always assuming of course that the plant when new was correctly engineered with the correct flame shape for a particular furnace.

Fuel Oil Composition

Fuel oil has been marketed for many years against a grading of viscosity based upon the Redwood Scale, i.e. 35, 200, 960 and 3,500 seconds No 1 at 100°F for different grades of fuel varying from

**TABLE 6.5: TYPICAL BURNER ATOMISING VISCOSITIES
QUOTED BY UK BURNER MANUFACTURERS**

Company	Atomiser type	Viscosity centistokes
Babcock	Steam atomised	25
	Air atomised	25
	Pressure Jet	20
Hamworthy	Rotary Cup	55-77
	Pressure Jet	15.5
	Steam atomised	15.5
	Air atomised	15.5
Laidlaw Drew	Air atomised	20
	Steam atomised	20
Nu-Way	Pressure Jet	15
Parkinson Cowan GWB Ltd	Air atomised	50
	Steam atomised	50
Peabody Holmes	Air atomised	15-20
	Steam atomised	20
	Pressure Jet	15
Saacke	Rotary Cup	60
NEI-Cochran	Pressure Jet	15-24

FIGURE 6.4: ATOMISING VISCOSITY AND STACK EMISSION

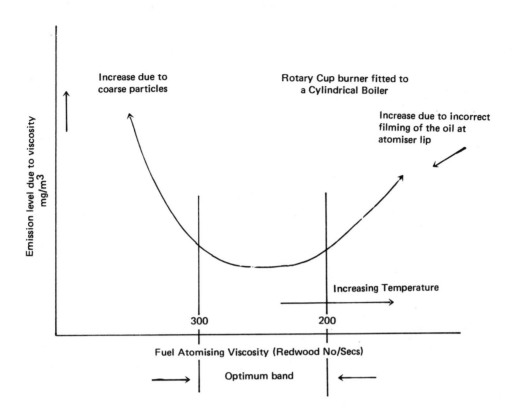

FIGURE 6.6: FLAME SHAPES AND EFFECTS IN THE COMBUSTION CHAMBER OF A FIRE TUBE BOILER

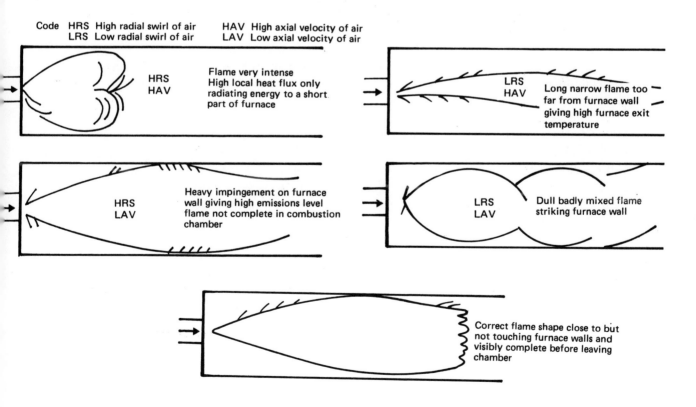

gas oil to heavy fuel oil. Heavy fuel oil is a mixture being the residue of the distillation process, mixed with a lighter oil to give 'pumpability'. Modern refinery processes have tended to produce heavy fuel oils somewhat higher in specific gravity and due to process techniques with heavier hydro carbon molecules broadly classed as asphaltenes. These asphaltenes require a longer combustion chamber residence time to burn out and so can bring about a higher emission of unburnt carbon from the plant if not correctly handled. Every care must be taken to ensure that the burner is efficient and that the correct atomisation viscosity is being maintained at the atomiser to give such fuels a chance to burn out completely.

Natural Gas Firing

Gas does not have the more obvious pollution problems associated with the combustion of heavy fuel oil. But care must be taken to ensure that combustion takes place with at least a small amount of excess air. Figure 6.8 illustrates graphically the problem. To the left of the central continuous line it can be seen how with a deficiency of air highly toxic carbon monoxide is being produced. With an oil burner this would manifest itself as black smoke from the chimney but this is not necessarily the case with gas. The colour of the flame may change to yellow from blue but this would be the only visual indication.

If the boiler plant is not gas tight and the products of combustion leak into the boiler house a serious health hazard would develop. A combustion test should always include a test for the presence of carbon monoxide whenever one is carrying out a check on excess air. The dotted line on Figure 6.8 shows the onset of carbon monoxide production in spite of excess air being present in the furnace. This is a burner design feature: the better the design, the closer should be the zero excess air point before carbon monoxide forms.

The Range of Combustion Equipment

Burners are devices for creating the necessary environment to allow a fuel to burn with stability and safety. Stability implies that the flame propogation will be allowed to proceed without fear of the flame being blown off the burner head. Safety implies that the flame will be controlled to burn in the direction it is intended and will not be allowed to deteriorate to such a condition that dangerous conditions arise and explosions are possible.

It can be seen therefore that a burner must have a construction to create a stable zone in which a flame can be established. Figure 6.9 shows a Hamworthy rotary cup burner designed to fire oil, gas and pulverised coal and illustrates the principle of recirculation around a burner atomiser to create a reversal zone for flame stabilisation.

Various forms of stabilisers or diffusers are used by burner manufacturers but the most important factor to look for in the design is that the flame stability is complete and yet an ample supply of combustion air is available to the centre of the flame. A shortage of air to the flame centre, will result in a dark centre to the flame with the formation of a finely divided soot or carbon. This cracking of the carbon particles in the flame is a consequence of pyrolosis which occurs when a hydrocarbon fuel is released in a high temperature zone without sufficient oxygen to allow complete combustion. This soot persists through the flame and once formed is difficult to burn off.

Once a flame has been established the next requirement is to ensure that the combustion air is fed into the flame in such a way as to ensure adequate mixing in an evenly distributed fashion. A flame in a combustion chamber as found in shell boilers must be centrally disposed in the flue tube. Mal- distribution of the combustion air to the flame will cause the flame to impinge on the furnace walls. These walls are relatively cold to the flame and any carbon particle which is burning progressively in the furnace will be chilled and extinguished. As noted previously a small cenosphere of coke will then pass through the boiler unburnt. This cenosphere obviously constitutes a fuel loss as well as a pollution hazard.

FIGURE 6.7: ASPHALTENES AND STACK EMISSION

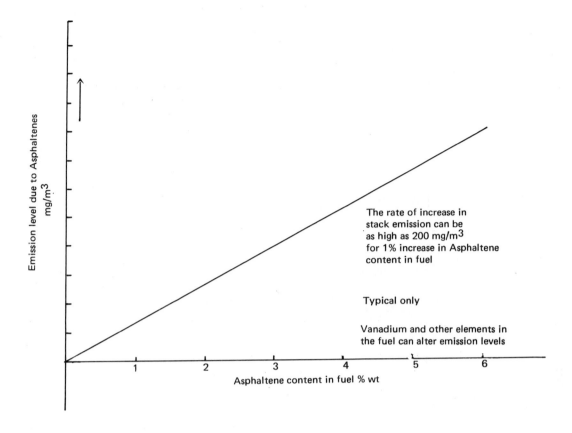

The rate of increase in
stack emission can be
as high as 200 mg/m³
for 1% increase in Asphaltene
content in fuel

Typical only

Vanadium and other elements in
the fuel can alter emission levels

**FIGURE 6.8: EXCESS AIR, CARBON DIOXIDE, OXYGEN AND CARBON MONOXIDE
IN NATURAL GAS COMBUSTION**

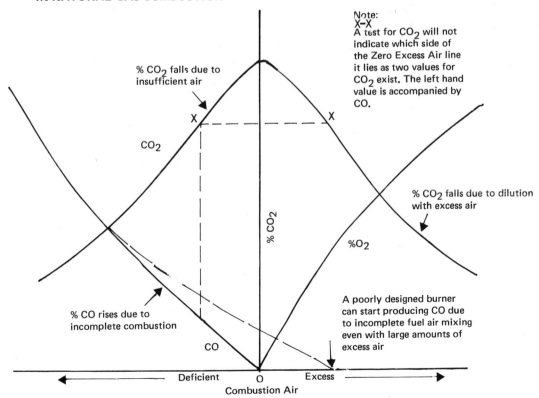

Note:
X-X
A test for CO_2 will not
indicate which side of
the Zero Excess Air line
it lies as two values for
CO_2 exist. The left hand
value is accompanied by
CO.

% CO_2 falls due to
insufficient air

% CO_2 falls due to dilution
with excess air

% CO rises due to
incomplete combustion

A poorly designed burner
can start producing CO due
to incomplete fuel air mixing
even with large amounts of
excess air

Note: When testing combustion conditions on gas fired plant always check for CO.

**FIGURE 6.9: SPECULATIVE FLAME STRUCTURE
PF FIRING WITH FUEL OIL**

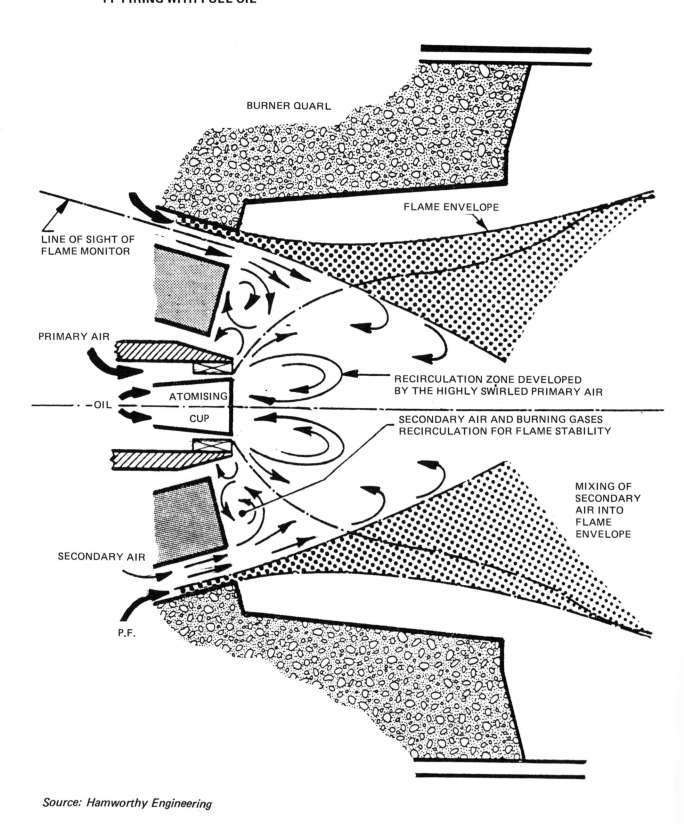

Source: Hamworthy Engineering

Such stack solids have been the subject of much research work over the last 20 years and great strides have been made to reduce the level of solid matter emitted from a chimney. Most of the development work to reduce this level has been directed towards improving air distribution to the flame front and the mixing and atomisation of the fuel. A prudent purchaser of new plant will always ascertain performance as to stack solids and excess air as shown in Figure 6.2. This curve is the performance blueprint to which a boiler/burner unit must be set up.

Fuel Oil Burners

Burners for fuel oil can be classified on a basis of the technique used to prepare the fuel for burning i.e. atomisation. The finer the fuel droplets are atomised the more readily will the particles come in contact with the oxygen in the air and burn. One can roughly say that the burn out time of a droplet of gas oil in a combustion chamber follows a 'd^2 law'. If one doubles the size of the droplet one needs four times the length of time to burn out the particle. With modern furnaces and heavier grades of fuel the need to produce consistently fine droplets cannot be over emphasised.

Atomisers can be divided into three main types:

Pressure Jet where the fuel is atomised by direct pressure forcing the oil through a swirling chamber and orifice to produce a conical spray pattern.

Twinfluid atomisers where a second fluid is used to effect the pulverisation of the fuel into fine particles. The second fluid is usually compressed air or steam. This type of atomiser needs further sub division into

   —low pressure air atomisation where, as the name implies, air at approximately 1,000mmWG is used

   —medium pressure air with air at 1-2 bar (14-30 psig)

   —high pressure air with air at 8-10 bar (100-150 psig)

   —steam atomisation using steam at a pressure ranging from 5 to 20 bar.

Rotary cup atomisers where a hollow cup is rotated at high speed (5,000 rpm). Oil is fed to the inside of the horizontally mounted atomiser cup and allowed to pass down the inclined sides of the cup to the cup edge where it forms a sheet or film and is struck by a high velocity air stream which atomises the fuel. (This type of burner can also be regarded as a twinfluid atomiser but for the sake of clarity it is probably best to keep the classification separate).

Variations on the burner types exist; the most popular being a pressure jet atomiser with a steam or air shroud to assist atomisation when the burner is turned down to a low output. With the pressure jet burner atomisation quality falls off very quickly if the pressure to the atomiser is reduced even slightly. The burner therefore has a poor turn down ratio and in order to eliminate this fault the twin fluid technique is employed at low oil pressures. The technique is not suitable for wide load changes on a constant basis as a point exists in the atomising range where atomisation falls off very badly.

The suitability of burner types of boiler plant is worthy of discussion.

If the long slender combustion chamber of a shell or packaged boiler is considered the conclusion must be drawn that a similar shape of flame, filling the furnace at full load yet not touching the cold walls, would be the ideal flame pattern. The choice of burner therefore is limited to those capable of this performance. Both the medium pressure air burner and the rotary cup are in this category and are capable, given the correct operating conditions, of a high level of performance. They are able to burn cleanly at quite low excess air levels, 15 to 20 per cent, and emit quite low amounts of unburnt carbon or stack solids.

When a larger combustion chamber is required, as found in larger water tube boilers, then the ideal arrangement for this type of plant is either pressure jet or steam atomisation with the latter being the preferred system. Combustion of the heavier grades of fuel oils is much facilitated by the use of a steam atomised burner. Recent development work has reduced the amount of steam used in atomising the fuel to a low value. In addition this type of burner has an exceedingly good turndown capability maintaining fine atomisation throughout the range.

The firing of furnaces as found in the glass and steel industries sometimes calls for a burner capable of firing under rather arduous conditions. This application tends to favour the more robust construction and inherent protection against the back radiation from a hot brick lined furnace of the low pressure air burner, a type not however likely to prove suitable for modern boiler plant.

Gas Burners

These are classified broadly into two categories, the internal or premix type and the external mix types. Again variations can be struck.

Internal or premix types are as the name implies burners where the gas and air are mixed prior to combustion.

The external or nozzle mix types allow the mixing to take place externally.

Most boiler plants are fired with the nozzle mix type, whilst some furnace applications use premix. In general it can be said that nozzle mix burners are quicker in operation and have a more stable start up condition. Figure 6.10 shows a modern nozzle mix combined oil and gas burner fitted with a steam atomised fuel oil system.

FIGURE 6.10: A COMBINED OIL/GAS BURNER

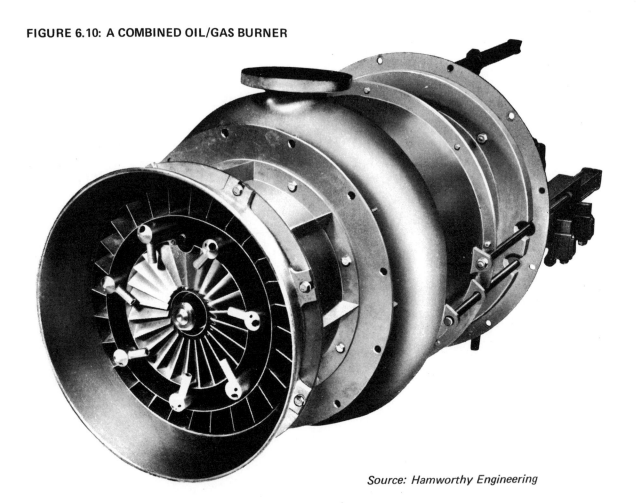

Source: Hamworthy Engineering

Flue Gas Analysis

The amount of excess air carried by a burner depends on three factors:

—the quality of the combustion equipment and its ability to present the fuel and air in such a fashion as to allow complete and thorough combustion

—the shape of the combustion chamber: a large chamber giving ample opportunity for mixing can operate with less excess air than the small combustion chambers normally found on a shell or packaged boiler

—the variation in combustion air supply due to changes in chimney draught with excess air used to ensure that the burner has enough combustion air to prevent smoke at the times of worst chimney draught.

The technique normally adopted by combustion engineers to assess combustion performance is to measure the amount of carbon dioxide present in the flue gas. As an example, a fuel oil having a carbon content of say 86 per cent will yield 16 per cent carbon dioxide in the flue gas should the burner be supplied with the exact amount of air required for combustion, i.e. at the stoichiometric point.

Returning to Figure 6.1, it can be seen that two volumes of flue gas are noted in Block A, namely the dry and wet gas samples. The wet gas sample is drawn from the gases produced as a mixture in the stack. The nitrogen shown in the sample is that left over after the oxygen has been consumed.

From this illustration it can be seen that were one to measure the amount of carbon dioxide a sample would need to be taken from the main gas stream and the water vapour would condense. In this case the volume of gas per unit of fuel burnt is smaller.

The gas in the stack is known as *wet gas* as the water vapour has not been condensed. The gas sampled externally with the water condensing as it cools in the sampling lines is generally termed the *dry gas* sample.

It is important to realise this difference and it can be appreciated from Figure 6.1 that the total unit volume will be smaller when the water vapour is removed and the value of the carbon dioxide will be larger when expressed as a percentage of the total.

Measuring the volume of carbon dioxide or the amount of unused oxygen is the standard method employed in determining the quantity of excess air. It can be seen from Figure 6.1 that in the case of zero excess air (Block A) a maximum reading for carbon dioxide could be taken depending on the fuel burnt. Equally no excess air would return a zero reading should an oxygen analyser be employed.

Figure 6.11 is a useful chart as it evaluates the percentage of excess air against carbon dioxide and oxygen readings.

Fuels vary in the weight ratio of hydrogen to carbon and so the amount of carbon dioxide produced in the combustion process will also vary. In practice a standard is taken which is based upon an average ratio and combustion data are produced around the 'standard' type of fuel. At best a combustion efficiency test based upon such standards is a compromise. If an accurate assessment of combustion performance is required, as for example during equipment acceptance trials, then an individual examination of the fuel's constituents will be necessary. Nevertheless Figure 6.11 does show the relationship between hydrogen—carbon ratios and excess air for most common fuels and can be used in general combustion efficiency testing.

Boiler/Burner Flue Gas Losses

British Standard Specification 845—(1972) sets out formulae to determine the amount of heat lost to the chimney based on standard grades of fuels. As noted earlier, the variation in fuel constituents renders a need for a base from which to calculate heat losses.

FIGURE 6.11: PROPERTIES OF PRODUCTS OF COMBUSTION

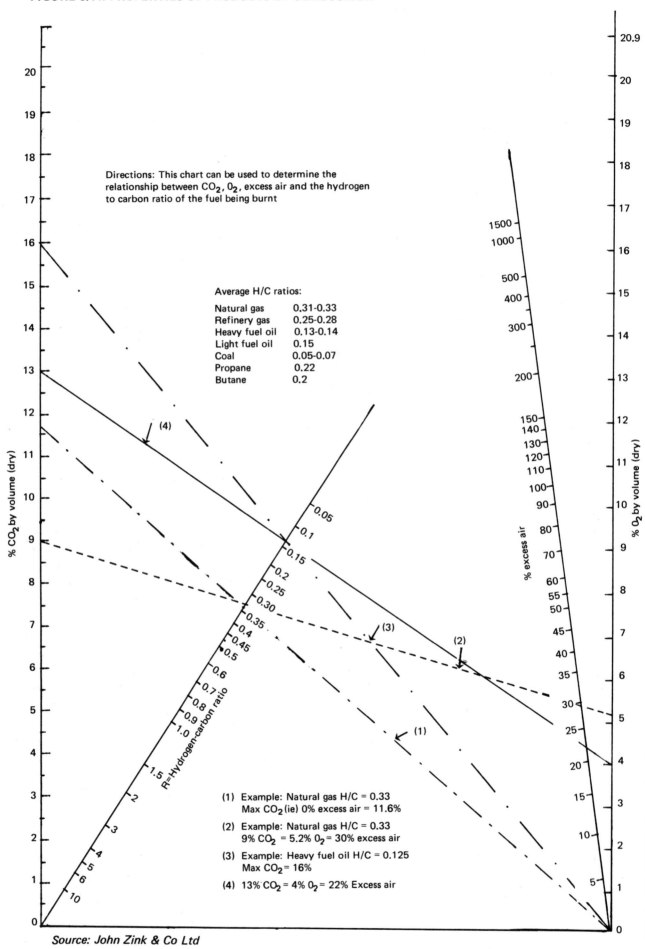

Directions: This chart can be used to determine the relationship between CO_2, O_2, excess air and the hydrogen to carbon ratio of the fuel being burnt

Average H/C ratios:

Natural gas	0.31-0.33
Refinery gas	0.25-0.28
Heavy fuel oil	0.13-0.14
Light fuel oil	0.15
Coal	0.05-0.07
Propane	0.22
Butane	0.2

(1) Example: Natural gas H/C = 0.33
    Max CO_2 (ie) 0% excess air = 11.6%

(2) Example: Natural gas H/C = 0.33
    9% CO_2 = 5.2% O_2 = 30% excess air

(3) Example: Heavy fuel oil H/C = 0.125
    Max CO_2 = 16%

(4) 13% CO_2 = 4% O_2 = 22% Excess air

% CO_2 by volume (dry)

% excess air

% O_2 by volume (dry)

R=Hydrogen-carbon ratio

Source: John Zink & Co Ltd

Heat losses to the stack can be graded into two components:

—that due to the sensible heat in the mass of the flue gas passing away

—the heat contained in the water vapour produced by the combustion of the hydrogen in the fuel. This water vapour contains the latent heat of vaporisation, i.e. the heat required to change water into its gaseous or steam phase. It is equal to approximately 1,000 Btu's/lb (2,226 kJ/kG) and is broadly termed the hydrogen loss.

Attention is also drawn at this stage to the fact that the calorific value of a fuel can be given in two ways: namely the gross calorific value (GCV) which represents all the heat given up by the fuel when it is burnt and the nett calorific value (NCV) which is equal to the GCV less the heat of vaporisation.

Boiler efficiency calculated with nett calorific value will give a higher figure and it is important to check when a boiler performance efficiency is quoted whether nett or gross calorific values have been quoted. Continental boiler makers tend to use nett values, which give higher thermal efficiency figures.

Sensible Heat Loss

To overcome the difficulty of calculating from first principles the weight of flue gas passing to the stack relative to the hydrogen/carbon ratio of the fuel, the British Standard allows the use of constants for the more common fuels used in industry. These constants for sensible heat loss are:

—bituminous coal   0.63 K_1 value for coal
—fuel oil   0.56 K_1 value for oil
—natural gas   0.38 K_1 value for gas

The formula used for calculating the sensible heat loss to the stack will be:

$$\%SHloss = \frac{K_1 \; (\text{Flue gas temp}^{\circ}C - \text{Air temp}^{\circ}C)}{\%CO_2}$$

This gives the value of heat loss as a percentage of the nett calorific value of the fuel. For the same loss based upon gross CV the above value must be multiplied by the ratio of nett CV to gross CV.

These ratios are: coal 0.9624; fuel oil 0.9395; natural gas 0.9231

The modern practice in flue gas analysis is to use an oxygen analyser. It has proven to be very reliable as a constant monitoring device. Two types are in use, one where the oxygen level in the stack is measured and the second where the gas to be tested is withdrawn from the flue system through a sampling line. The former is a wet gas sample, i.e. contains water vapour in a gaseous form, the latter is a dry gas sample where the water has been condensed.

Most charts and combustion efficiency assessment aids are based upon dry gas samples and it is these values that are referred to in this chapter.

If a percentage oxygen reading is taken the formula can be modified both for the oxygen reading (instead of carbon dioxide) and the correction factor for the NCV/GCV factor. The new constants are derived by using the same CV ratios as set out above.

The relationship between percentage carbon dioxide and percentage oxygen can be expressed as:

$$\%CO_2 = \frac{(20.9 - \%O_2) \times \%CO_2 \text{ max}}{20.9}$$

$\%CO_2$ max is the percentage in a flue gas sample without any excess air being present, i.e. the stoichiometric ratio. These values for the standard fuels are—coal 18 per cent, fuel oil 15.6 per cent, natural gas 11.9 per cent.

The formula can therefore be arranged to give:

$\%CO_2 = 0.86\ (20.9-\%O_2)$ for coal
$\%CO_2 = 0.74\ (20.9-\%O_2)$ for fuel oil
$\%CO_2 = 0.57\ (20.9-\%O_2)$ for natural gas

Combining coefficients and using O_2 values the sensible heat loss based upon the GCV of the fuel can be calculated using K_1 values:

−coal: $\%$ loss $= K_1\ (T_G-T_A)/(20.9-\%O_2)$
−fuel oil: $\%$ loss $= K_1\ (T_G-T_A)/(20.9-\%O_2)$
−natural gas: $\%$ loss $= K_1\ (T_G-T_A)/(20.9-\%O_2)$

where T_G = Flue gas temp $^{\circ}$C, T_A = Air temp $^{\circ}$C in the boiler house, K_1 for coal = 0.705, K_1 for fuel oil =0.711, K_1 for natural gas = 0.615. .

Heat Loss Due to Hydrogen and Moisture

The additional loss which has to be added to the sensible heat loss is the one due to the hydrogen in the fuel requiring energy for its vapour phase. The British Standard caters for this loss in a rather lengthy formula. The loss due to hydrogen and moisture in fuel based upon GCV of fuel is equal to:

$$\frac{H_2O\ in\ fuel\ \%\ wt + 9H_2\ in\ fuel\ \%\ wt\ (2460 - 4.2\ Air\ temp\ ^{\circ}C + 2.1\ Flue\ gas\ temp\ ^{\circ}C)}{Gross\ Calorific\ Value\ of\ Fuel\ KJ/Kg}$$

The above formula can be simplified to suit the boiler house engineer by making assumptions as to the fuel properties.

Percentage loss due to hydrogen and moisture $= K_2\ (1121.4 + (Flue\ gas\ temp\ ^{\circ}C-Air\ temp\ ^{\circ}C))$

where K_2 for fuel oil   = 0.0051
and K_2 for natural gas   = 0.0083

The moisture loss from coal can vary from delivery to delivery and in the author's opinion should involve a closer assessment. However one company, Neotronics Ltd, manufacturer of a complete sampling probe system which incorporates a microprocessor to evaluate stack loss, has given a value based upon their experience of 0.00409 as the K_2 factor for coal and assumes 15 per cent moisture on the coal.

Combining the two losses into one formula we have:

Stack Loss $\%$ = $\%$ Sensible Heat Loss + $\%$ Hydrogen and Moisture Loss

$$= \frac{K_1\ (T_G-T_A)}{(20.9-\%O_2)} + K_2\ (1121.4 + (T_G-T_A))$$

where T_G = Flue gas temp $^{\circ}$C, T_A = Air temp $^{\circ}$C, K_1 = Sensible Heat Loss Constant, K_2 = Hydrogen and Moisture Loss.

Calculating Boiler Efficiency

From an assessment of the loss of heat up the chimney and an assumption as to the amount of heat escaping from the boiler casing and lagging—usually three per cent of the full load of the boiler—one can, by subtraction arrive at a boiler efficiency:

$\%$ Boiler efficiency = 100−(Stack loss + RUA loss)

If a blow down device for boiler water purity control is in use then an estimate will have to be made as to this loss and added to the other losses. It should be remembered that the R and UA Loss (Radiation and Unaccounted Loss) is given at full boiler output, i.e. three per cent of full boiler load. This loss which is constant regardless of boiler output, becomes six per cent when the boiler is running at half load and 12 per cent at a quarter load. This much overlooked fact illustrates the sense in running boilers at maximum output and not having several boilers feeding into a main at low outputs. Figures 6.12 to 6.14 are given as a quick guide to flue gas losses.

Installing a Combustion Control System

The decision to proceed with the installation of a combustion control system will depend upon the plant being able to run satisfactorily at the lower level of excess air, thereby effecting a fuel saving. This decision is a vital one, and the preceding text has set out the points to look out for.

Gas and light oil should present little difficulty in conversion, providing the boiler equipment will perform to the tighter limits. In this direction it is prudent to run the plant on hand control for a few days, carefully monitoring the plant's performance. To cut down the air supply to a burner for a few minutes to prove a point is not to be compared to say running it in that fashion for a few days. Such difficulties as boiler tube fouling and carbon formation on the furnace walls will not become apparent until several hours of operation on the lower air level.

If the plant can be shown to run at a lower air level it is recommended that the performance be compared with the ideal case as shown in Figure 6.15. The information given here is based on the author's observation of boiler plant over the past 20 years. Types of boilers are identified but mention cannot be made of specific burner combinations for obvious reasons.

Prospective clients of combustion control equipment manufacturers should ask their intended suppliers to provide them with performance data after this fashion, and the generosity of the author's demands should mean that his performance criteria should be bettered. But, do not forget to ask questions as to how stack solids level will alter when a new combustion control system is fitted. It is no good at all to have 10 per cent excess air level on a highly rated combustion chamber to find the Clean Air man banging at the boiler house door.

Finally in this section a word about the turndown ratio. The turndown ratio of a burner is dependent mainly upon the burner's ability to maintain a stable flame when the fuel and air flows are reduced. Gas burners can turn down to very small flames quite satisfactorily, whereas oil burners find this somewhat more difficult to do.

Be wary of extravagant claims on the part of burner makers to large turndown ratios. Invariably, these claims are accompanied by a profound omission on the part of the claimant to mention how enormous becomes the excess air at the lower firing rate. It is a fundamental law of fluid flow that through a given flow opening the air volume passing varies as the square root of the pressure drop across that hole. This means basically, that if one wishes to produce a turndown of air flow say 10 to 1, the pressure drop across the air supply hole or quarl to the burner has to be in the ratio of 100 to 1. Imagine the case—a burner with full load wind-box pressure of say 100 mm —a reasonable figure—with a 10 to 1 turndown. To maintain the same ratio of oil to air, the wind-box would have to reduce to 1 mm WG, a totally uncontrollable figure of minute proportions. In consequence the burner, in such cases, usually runs with a higher windbox pressure and in fact a considerable amount of excess air.

If one tries to control automatically at these levels of windbox pressure 1 mm WG, it is asking a great deal from the control mechanism, and great care must be taken in these cases to ensure the plant continues to function after the commissioning engineer has left.

Combustion Control Equipment

The technique of combustion control in the past has been one based upon some form of a cam control to regulate the relative flow openings of an oil valve with respect to an air damper or vice

FIGURE 6.12: FLUE GAS LOSSES—GAS OIL

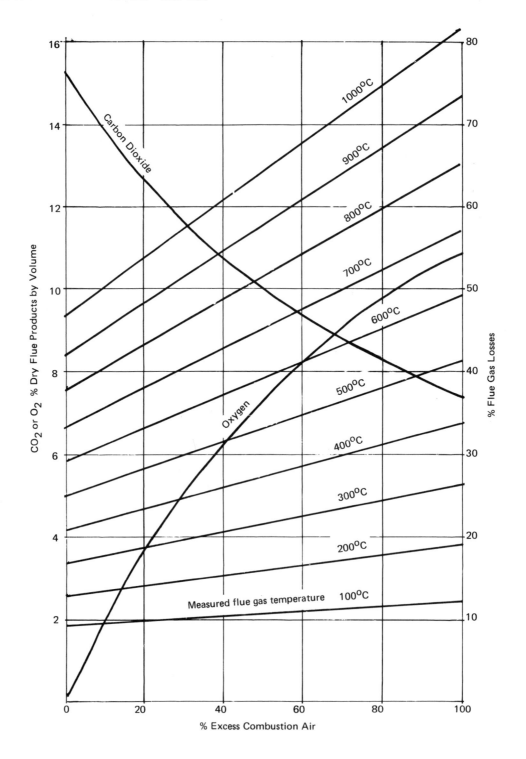

Based on gross calorific value and an ambient temperature of 20°C

Source: Department of Energy

FIGURE 6.13: FLUE GAS LOSSES—HEAVY FUEL OIL

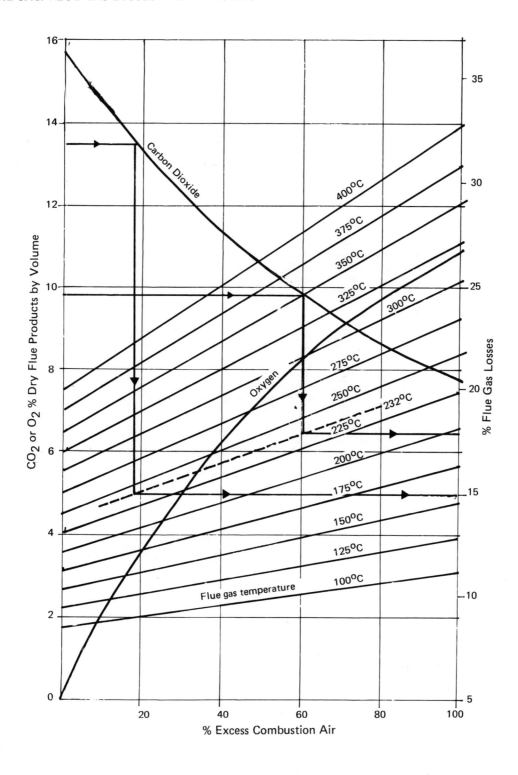

Based on gross calorific value and an ambient temperature of 20ºC

Source: Department of Energy

FIGURE 6.14: FLUE GAS LOSSES—NATURAL GAS

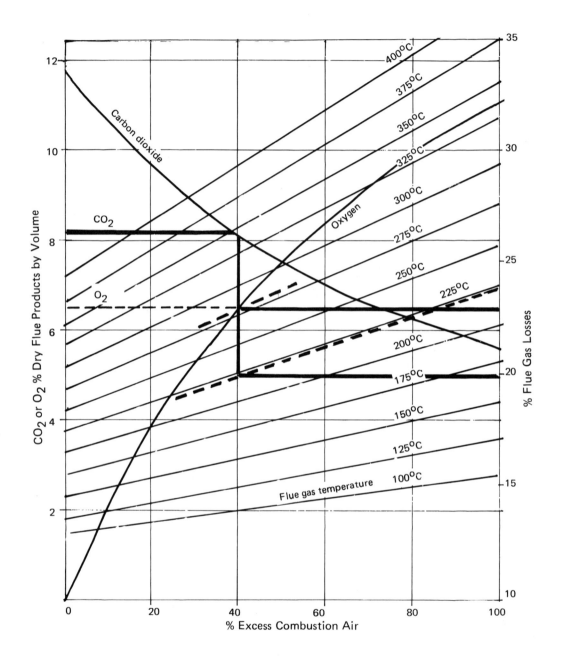

Example: Flue gas sample reads 8.2% CO_2 Stack gas
Temperature 280°C Flue gas loss = 23%
Stack temp. 220°C Flue gas loss = 20%
Reading must intercept CO_2 or O_2 curve whichever is taken

Source: Department of Energy

versa, the metering was entirely dependent on mechanically set conditions. Some more elaborate systems actually attempted to measure air flow by measuring the pressure drop across an orifice or some other part of the air flow system and as this was related to the flow by a square law, a device was used to extract the square root of this signal and use it to control the oil flow. This system in fact is used on very large boiler plants quite satisfactorily and has been updated to take corrections to flow conditions by measuring how much excess oxygen exists in the flue products.

It is, perhaps, in this direction that the biggest steps forward have been made in combustion control, the so called oxygen feedback system, and this has been made much more of a reliable control system by the increased use of oxygen analysers employing zirconium oxide sensors.

In the past the measurement of excess air in the stack was carried out by either measuring the volume of carbon dioxide produced or by the amount of free oxygen existing in the chimney flue gases. It was seen in Figure 6.11 that these are related. The carbon dioxide method, whilst splendid for a 'one time shot' type of operation as found during boiler testing, does not lend itself to continuous sampling. Boiler plants have therefore tended to go towards the oxygen level measurement system and a paramagnetic system was used to measure the oxygen content. This system is basically one which relies upon the effect a magnetic field has upon the migration of oxygen molecules in a gas stream, by allowing the field to divert the oxygen across an element a degree of cooling of the resistive element took place and this change in temperature producing a change in resistance was used to produce a reading of oxygen.

A possible drawback with this otherwise quite reliable system is its response time and furthermore as they are necessarily low oxygen concentrations the signal from the cell is at its lowest under such conditions and can provide a sluggish response to change.

The fact that zirconium oxide when seeded with something like lime or yttria had the amazing property of becoming a fuel cell in the presence of oxygen brought about its development as a probe for oxygen measurement in flues.

TABLE 6.15: PERFORMANCE EXPECTATIONS FOR BOILER PLANT

Performance expectations for boiler plant fitted with automatic air/fuel ratio along with burners designed to meet the Clean Air Act.

Lancashire Boilers

As the Combustion Chamber Heat Release Rate (CCHRR) is low—no trouble with Stack Solids (SS). Brick Setting makes air ingress possible and accurate oxygen sampling impossible. Sampling at end of combustion chamber only accurate method. System needs two probes, one per flue. Best Excess Air say 20 per cent. SS less than 0.2 per cent—on gas burning check for carbon monoxide at combustion chamber exit. Boiler Efficiency (BE) 70-75 per cent.

Economic Boilers Dry Back (Circa 1940)

Low CCHRR—no SS problems usually run under suction in the furnace. Oxygen sampling difficult but can be engineered to be fairly gastight—then performance can be SS 0.2 per cent 20 per cent Excess Air 75 per cent BE.

Economic Boilers Wet Back (Pre 1950)

Less chance of air ingress with this type of plant provided maintenance is good. Should run at 15 per cent Excess Air 0.2 per cent SS 78 per cent BE.

Package Boilers

Wide variety of home and foreign types. Check CCHRR of OK aim for better than 15 per cent Excess Air using Figure 6.2 as guide to keep plant legal. BE should be better than 80 per cent.

Note

Careful consideration should be given to any scheme involving twin flue boilers with a common combustion chamber. The sampling of the gas in the stack will not indicate the exact excess air conditions in each flue but simply an average value of the two readings.

FIGURE 6.16: OXYGEN FEEDBACK COMBUSTION CONTROL SYSTEM

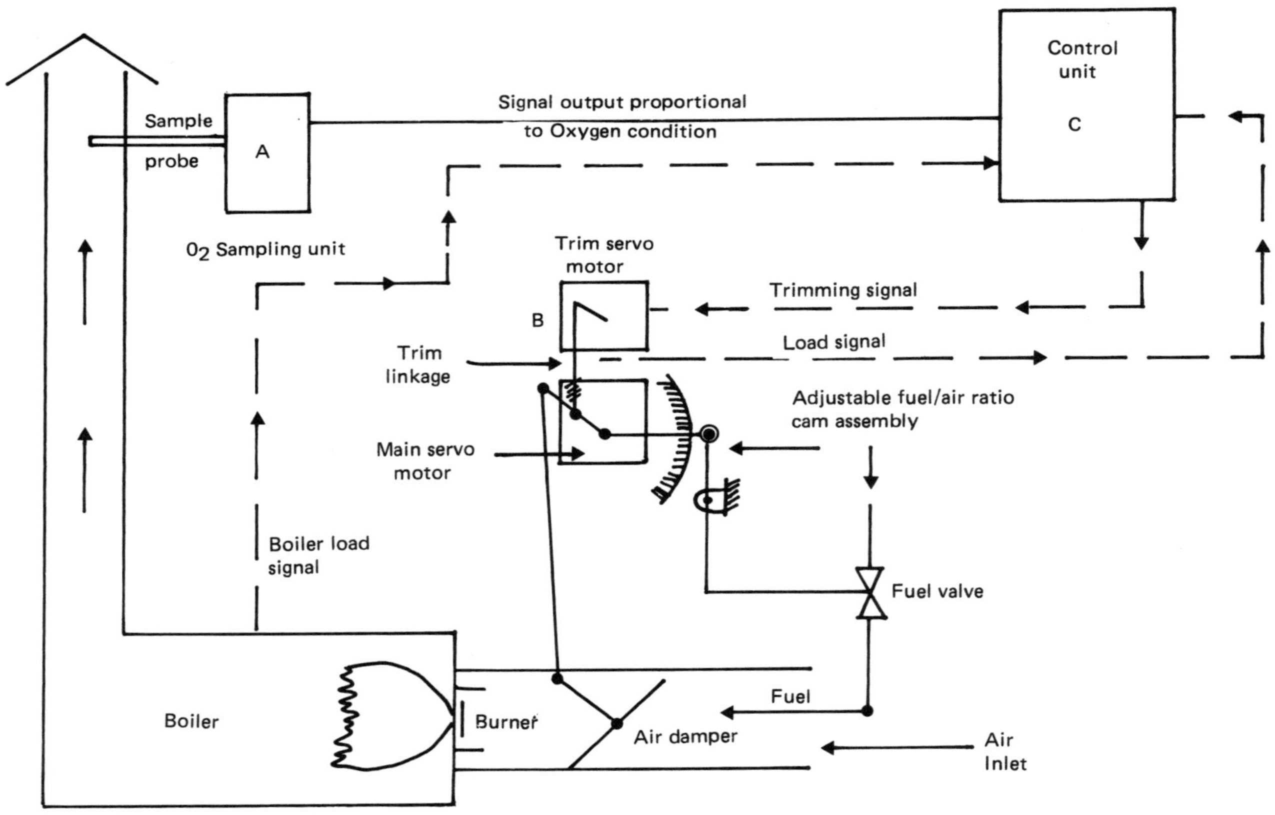

If a flat disc of zirconium oxide covered with a fine platinum mesh is heated to 700°C and placed such that one side of the disc is in contact with the atmosphere and the other side with the flue gas, a voltage will be developed across that cell which is proportional to the partial pressures of the oxygen. In other words, the smaller the oxygen level in the stack the bigger the signal: the atmosphere being fairly constant in oxygen level at about 21 per cent.

This voltage can now be used to control the air or fuel flow system with the distinct advantage that a speedy response to an oxygen level change in the stack takes place.

A control system functioning on the oxygen system is shown graphically in Figure 6.16.

The unit, mounted on or near the chimney, draws flue gas across the zirconia cell which is held at a temperature of about 700°C in a specially constructed oven with precise temperature control. The products of combustion, once sampled, are returned to the stack where they join the main flue gas stream to atmosphere. This method of sampling ensures a measure of safety, as if the heated cell of 700°C was placed directly in the flue it may act as an ignition source, should inflammable gases be present in the flue, as might happen should a plant suddenly shut down under a component failure. By placing the cell outside the stack sampling velocities and antiflash devices can be built into the design to preclude the chances of an explosion.

The signal from the stack unit A is passed to the control box C where it is processed electronically to a form which will move the trim damper control to increase or decrease combustion air dependent upon the set point adjustment for oxygen level.

The trim system is recommended for control as from the Figure it can be seen that the course setting of the air fuel ratio system ensures that an air fuel ratio having excess air characteristics is always in operation and a final trimming of the air is carried out by control motor B. In the event of a sampling system failure the coarse control would ensure that smoke was not produced by an oil burner or heavy carbon monoxide by a gas burner.

Scope for Cost Saving

By operating a boiler plant and using an air fuel ratio controller the improved control of excess air should show a saving on fuel consumption.

If one assumes a constant stack temperature it can be shown that for each two per cent reduction in oxygen content the combustion efficiency of the plant increases by about one per cent. This reduction in excess air usually means an increase in flame temperature with a greater transfer of heat taking place in the furnace, with a consequent reduction in flue gas temperature in the stack. It should be remembered that furnace temperature radiation transfer varies according to the Stefan Boltzman formula and is to the fourth power of the temperature. A small increase in flame temperature due to reducing excess air in the furnace, brings about a bigger benefit of transfer rate in the furnace—to the fourth power!

Reducing air flow on large plants also reduces fan loads. It can be safely assumed that the reductions outlined above of one per cent will rise to two per cent if these are taken into account.

As shown earlier, the expectations are that natural gas plant can be run at a one to two per cent oxygen level and a heavy oil plant at between two and a half and three and a half per cent oxygen.

Finally, however, it should be remembered that any combustion control system will only control a burner to its best performance. It cannot make a badly designed burner into a well designed unit!

7

ENERGY MANAGEMENT IN LIGHTING

Victor Neal and Michael Wells

Good energy and cost management in lighting needs to fulfil two objectives:

—to ensure that the lighting provided is sufficient and suitable for the purpose, and

—to obtain the required lighting result in the most energy effective manner practicable.

A closer look at these two objectives is taken in the first part of the chapter. The range of lamps available to industry and commerce is reviewed in terms of efficacy and suitability for use in both new lighting installations and as more economical alternatives to less efficient lamp types already in use. Other subejcts covered include luminaires, maintenance, controls and the importance of planning for the lighting requirement at the design stage. A brief bibliography of useful publications on lighting and lighting management is given at the end.

Providing Sufficient and Suitable Lighting

The quantity and quality of lighting provided is fundamental to peoples' ability to carry out visual tasks with speed and accuracy. Good energy management must therefore take into account the influence lighting exerts on productivity and hence on the total level of energy consumption relative to output.

Lighting may account for only three per cent of the total amount of energy consumed in a factory but if that lighting is insufficient or unsuitable productivity will suffer. If this is the case then part of the remaining 97 per cent of energy consumed—for process and space heating, etc—will necessarily be wasted.

The same method of assessing overall energy and cost effectiveness in commercial premises—shops, offices, etc (where lighting may account for 25 or 30 per cent of the total energy consumption)—also reveals the need to ensure that the standards of lighting employed are in accord with the visual requirements.

The economic benefit of providing at least the recommended standards of lighting to achieve required or improved levels of productivity is more apparent when lighting costs are compared with other financial parameters. For example, the total lighting cost in office accommodation is usually between a half to one per cent of the wage and salary bill or the same percentages of added value in manufacturing premises.

Any doubts as to how much light is sufficient, or the requirements for lighting to be suitable, can be dispelled by referring to the CIBS' Code for Interior Lighting. In addition to detailing the various quality requirements this code includes a schedule of recommended illuminances for a wide range of lighting applications. These take account of the need for energy conservation, the higher cost of electricity relative to other fuels and the need for lighting to be cost effective. Parts of this schedule are summarised in Table 7.1 which provides some guidance on this subject.

The four key rules of good lighting practice are:

—ensure that there is sufficient light

—that it is of the right colour

TABLE 7.1: RECOMMENDED SERVICE ILLUMINANCES

For complete schedule refer to IES (CIBS) Code for Interior Lighting, 1977

Range	Code Illuminance (lux)	Examples of area of activity
General lighting for rooms and areas used either in-frequently and/or casual or simple visual tasks	20	Minimum service illuminance in exterior circulation areas
	30	Outdoor stores, stockyards
	50	Exterior walkways and platforms; indoor carparks
	75	Docks and quays
	100	Theatres and concert halls; hotel bedrooms, bathrooms
	150	Circulation areas in industry, stores and stock rooms
General lighting for interiors	200	Minimum service illuminance on the task
	300	Rough bench and machine work; general processes in chemical and food industries; casual reading and filing activities
	500	Medium bench and machine work; motor vehicle assembly; printing machine rooms, general offices, shops and stores. Retail sales areas
	750	Proof reading; general drawing offices; offices with business machines
	1,000	Fine bench and machine work; office machine assembly; colour work, critical drawing tasks
	1,500	Very fine bench and machine work; instrument and small precision mechanism assembly, electronic components, gauging and inspection of small intricate parts. May be partly provided by local lighting
Additional localised lighting for visually exacting tasks	2,000	Minutely detailed and precise work, e.g. very small parts of instruments, watch making and engraving; operating area in operating theatres. 2,000 lux minimum.

Source: Chartered Institution of Building Services

–that it is coming from suitable directions, and

–that it is falling on the actual working plane.

Compliance with these will ensure that the first objective of energy and cost management in lighting is met.

Obtaining Lighting in the Most Energy-Effective Manner

As the cost of the electricity consumed is usually the largest single cost element within the total cost of lighting it follows that, in general terms, the most energy effective lighting installation to provide the required lighting result will also be the most cost effective.

As a simple example of the significance of the electrical energy cost of lighting, consider a 100 watt GLS filament lamp which, in its average rated life of 1,000 hours, will consume 100 kWh of electricity. If the cost of electricity is 4p per kWh then the cost of the electricity consumed is £4.00 whereas the lamp cost is only 30p. Expressed another way, the electricity cost is 93 per cent of the total lamp plus energy cost.

Even when the capital costs of the lighting installation are included, the electricity cost is still the major cost element—usually between 50 and 80 per cent of total lighting cost. (Figure 7.2). Hence the relationship between energy and cost effectiveness which means that the need to ensure that lighting is as efficient as practicable in addition to being sufficient and suitable is paramount.

FIGURE 7.2: COST ELEMENTS OF A MERCURY FLUORESCENT (MBF/U) LIGHTING INSTALLATION

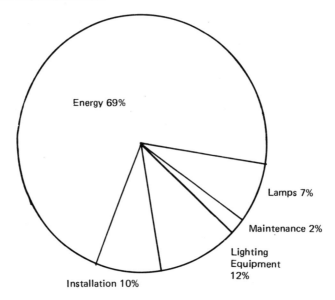

Selecting the Appropriate Light Source

The fundamental requirement, if lighting is to be as energy and cost effective as possible, is that the lamp type used for each application is the most efficient available within the parameters of suitability.

The efficacy of a lamp is expressed in terms of lumens per watt. (A lumen is a unit of light). And the efficacies of the various lamp types available vary considerably, by a factor of 10 to 1 or more. But, in some situations, the most efficient type may not be suitable.

The suitability of a lamp type for any application may depend upon several characteristics. The most important is the colour of the light provided by the lamp. For example, the most efficient lamp type—low pressure sodium—emits light of a colour which does not allow colours of objects to be recognised. Nevertheless it is suitable for those lighting applications where the recognition of colours is unnecessary.

Table 7.3 lists the various lamp types used for general lighting, the range of efficacies within each type and typical applications for which they are suitable.

Many existing lighting installations continue to use relatively inefficient lamps for which there are more efficient suitable alternatives. In some instances the change to using more efficient lamp types involves little or no capital expenditure so that the financial benefits of saving energy start immediately. In other cases some capital outlay will be required but the pay-back periods are relatively short and any such expenditure is usually a good investment.

Again consider the example of a 100 Watt GLS filament lamp and compare its energy consumption and cost with those of a 600 mm (two feet) 20 Watt fluorescent tube for say 3,000 hours operation. This would be typical for one year in many situations. Such a comparison for one lighting point only is shown in Table 7.4 and indicates a saving in energy cost, by using a 20 Watt fluorescent tube, of £8.64 per 3,000 hours per point. Lamp prices have not been included as they are virtually the same in each case and relatively insignificant.

Another often appropriate example is the comparison of costs of tungsten halogen (T/H) as against high pressure sodium (SON/T) lamps in area lighting or floodlighting installations. Table 7.5 compares the energy cost of a 1,000 Watt T/H lamp with that of a 250 Watt SON/T lamp for 2,000 hours or a typical one year's operation from dusk to midnight. Lamp costs are almost exactly the same for each type and therefore omitted.

Many industrial medium and high-bay lighting installations continue to use mercury fluorescent (MBF/U and MBFR/U) lamps and will have an apportionment of lighting costs similar to that shown in Figure 7.2. A more efficient lamp type for such situations is high pressure sodium which will result in the comparative cost elements illustrated in Figure 7.6. As the total value of each of these two diagrams is the same, the cost saving benefit resulting from the use of high pressure sodium lamps is included in Figure 7.6.

The principal energy saving developments in respect of fluorescent tubes have been the introduction of:

—fluorescent tubes which combine high efficacy and good colour rendering

—krypton filled lower wattage tubes, for switch-start circuits only, in specific ratings and colours

—compact fluorescent lamps as energy/cost saving alternatives to the lower wattage (40-100 W) GLS filament lamps.

The first two developments have, in energy and economic terms, created a preference for ratings and colours of fluorescent tubes. The following details of first and second choice ratings and colours, together with answers to some of the most frequent questions regarding these developments, have been extracted from the LIF (Lighting Industry Federation) Factfinder No.3 'Lamp Guide' and are reproduced in Table 7.7.

Compatibility

Fluorescent Lamps

When considering an existing installation in regard to fluorescent, say, changing to the Krypton filled lamps, it is necessary to check interchangeability. Some useful information on the compatibility of tubular fluorescent lamps is given in the first part of Table 7.8.

Discharge Lamps

The second part of Table 7.8 is devoted to these lamps. It summarises the various ranges of lamps and outlines the family of high and low pressure sodium lamps. It explains the types that are

TABLE 7.3: THE RANGE OF LAMP TYPES

Lamp Type	Typical * Efficiency L/W	Typical Applications
Low Pressure Sodium	70—145	Road lighting, security, area lighting (poor colour rendering)
High Pressure Sodium	51—110	Medium and high bay industrial, road and area lighting
Modern Fluorescent	35—72	In factories, offices, shops, hotels, restaurants and some domestic applications
Metal Halide	60—80	Floodlighting of sports stadia and arenas; high bay industrial and studio lighting; commercial lighting
Mercury Fluorescent	30—55	Industrial and road lighting, some commercial applications
Compact Fluorescent	35—50	Comparable to low wattage tungsten lamps. Applications as for tungsten GLS
Mercury blended	10—25	Used mainly as a plug-in replacement for tungsten GLS where a longer life is required
Tungsten Halogen	17—22	Floodlighting, display lighting, projectors and vehicle lighting
Tungsten GLS etc.	9—19	Domestic and many amenity type applications in commerce and industry. Display lighting

*   Efficiency in lumens per watt calculated from lighting design lumens and typical total circuit watts, i.e. including control gear losses for fluorescent and discharge lamps.

N.B. The actual efficiencies of specific lamp types and ratings may vary from the guide values quoted depending upon a) the wattage and b) the control gear losses.

TABLE 7.4: ENERGY COST COMPARISON, 100W GLS v 20W FLUORESCENT

Lamp Type	100W GLS	600mm 20W Fluorescent
Lighting Design Lumens	1200	1200
Circuit Watts	100W	28W
Energy Consumed per 3000 hours	300 kWh	84 kWh
Cost of energy consumed per 3000h @ 4p per kWh	£12.00	£3.36
Saving in energy cost per 3000h		£8.64

TABLE 7.5: ENERGY COST COMPARISON, 1000W TUNGSTEN HALOGEN (T/H) v HIGH PRESSURE SODIUM (SON/T)

Lamp Type	1,000W T/H	250W SON/T
Lighting Design Lumens	22,000	25,000
Circuit Watts	1,000	280
Energy Consumed per 2000 hours	2,000 kWh	560 kWh
Cost of energy consumed per 2000h @ 4p per kWh	£80.00	£28.00
Saving in energy cost per 2,000h		£52.00

N.B. In the case of dusk to dawn operation the operating hours are 4,000 per annum and annual saving is therefore doubled.

FIGURE 7.6: COST ELEMENTS OF A SODIUM LIGHTING INSTALLATION

Producing the Same Illuminance as the Mercury Fluorescent Installation in Figure 7.2

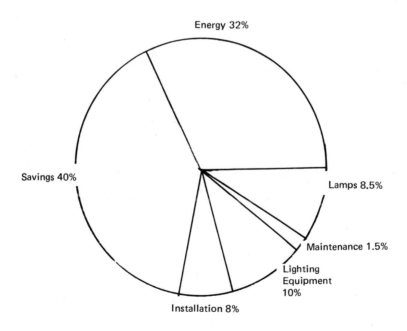

TABLE 7.7: TUBULAR FLUORESCENT LAMPS
Lengths and Ratings

LENGTH	FIRST CHOICE —for new luminaires —for replacement where circuit suitable KRYPTON-filled Energy-Saving 26mm (1″) dia. and 100W 38mm (1½″) dia.	SECOND CHOICE —where necessary for replacement ARGON-filled 38mm (1½″) dia.
2400mm (8ft)	100W (38mm dia.)	125W
1800mm (6ft)	70W 75/85W* (38mm dia.)	85W
1500mm (5ft)	58W	65/80W
1200mm (4ft)	36W	40W
600mm (2ft)	18W	20W

Other Current Types	Miniature U-Bend	Circular Compact	
Obsolescent Types			BC. Reflector. MCFA 40W 300mm (2ft) 85W 2400mm (8ft)

*75/85w Argon-filled on 75w ballast is an alternative to the 70w Krypton-filled lamp.

Features

The light output comes from phosphors which convert energy from a low pressure mercury discharge. The spectral light distribution is 'tailored' by the lamp designer, by mix of phosphors.

Operation position	Any	Restarting	Prompt
Control gear	Yes	Colour temperature (k)	Wide Range
Starting	Prompt	Colour rendering	Wide Range

Choice of Length and Rating

The principal lamps for lighting installations are listed in the Table. The original lamps were argon-filled 38mm diameter, and are retained for Starterless circuits. The modern range of krypton-filled lamps with 26mm diameter, and 100W 38mm diameter, should be first choice for Switch Start circuits. They offer energy saving, and increased LOR (light output ratio) for many luminaires.

Other Types

Other 26mm dia. lamps are available, and a range of miniature fluorescent lamps (4W–13W) with 16mm dia. There are also other shapes, e.g. Circular, U-Bend. Compact lamps with integral control gear are becoming available as GLS lamp replacements.

Table 7.7: Tubular Fluorescent Lamps (Cont)

Colours

COLOUR APPEARANCE	FIRST CHOICE—new installations and group replacement		SECOND CHOICE —matching in spot replacement	
(Nominal colour temperature)	*TRIPHOSPHORS* *Deluxe* *High Output*	*ORDINARY PHOSPHORS* *High Output* *Krypton-filled 26mm (1") dia. and 100W 38mm (1½") dia.* | *Argon-filled 38mm (1½") dia.*	*ORDINARY PHOSPHORS DeLuxe Argon-filled 38mm (1½") dia.*

COOL APPEARANCE (4000K SECTOR)
 	
WORK AREAS
e.g. offices, shops, factories
	TRIPHOSPHOR AT 4000K
	e.g.
	   Colour 84
	   Polylux 4000
	   Energy Saver 184
		COOL WHITE		NATURAL

(3500K) Packs/General	e.g. *Polylux 3500*	WHITE		

WARM APPEARANCE (3000K SECTOR)
 	
SOCIAL AREAS
e.g. restaurants, hotels the home
	TRIPHOSPHOR AT 3000K
	e.g.
	   Colour 83
	   Polylux 3000
	   Energy Saver 183
		WARM WHITE		W.W. DELUXE

Other Ordinary Phosphors	NORTHLIGHT (COL. MATCHING) for colour matching Kolorite/Trucolor for DHSS and Art Galleries			

Proprietary names of colours are in italics

Colour Range

The principal 'white' colours are listed in the Table. In the past, for a given colour appearance (e.g. warm), one had to choose between high output (e.g. Warm White) and improved colour rendering (e.g. Warm White Deluxe).

Modern phosphors (Tri-phosphors) combine very high output with deluxe rendering. They are especially suited to 26mm diameter lamps, since they are more temperature stable than ordinary phosphors, and have a lower depreciation rate.

Choice of Colours

First determine the appropriate colour appearance (cool or warm). A Tri-phosphor colour should then be first choice, preferably in 26mm diameter: high-output ordinary phosphors also are available in 26mm dia. and white is the colour usually included in packs. Deluxe ordinary phosphors are not suited to 26mm dia. lamps and will become less common.

Other Colours

The Table includes some colours for specialist applications. Lamps are also available with special phosphors, e.g. for use in printing machines.

Source: Lighting Industry Federation

TABLE 7.8: INTERCHANGEABILITY OF LAMPS

Tubular Fluorescent Lamps

First Choice Fluorescent Lamps

The new Krypton-filled lamps were developed in response to the need for energy-saving fluorescent lamps. They should be treated as First Choice both for new installations and for replacement in Switch Start luminaires. The following Technical Notes take the form of answers to common questions.

1. Which are the Krypton-filled Lamps?

26 mm (1 inch) Diameter	18W 600 mm (2 ft)	36W 1200 mm (4 ft)
	58W 1500 mm (5 ft)	70W 1800 mm (6 ft)
38 mm (1½ inch) Diameter	100W 2400 mm (8 ft)	

The caps have the normal bi-pin arrangement and fit standard bi-pin lampholders.

2. For What Circuits are they Suitable?

Krypton-filled lamps for use in switch start circuits, with flow-type starters. For technical reasons they are not for use on starterless circuits including dimming circuits. They are also not suitable for use with electronic starters, unless such starters are appropriately marked.

3. For What Ambient Conditions are they Suitable?

The same limits apply as for argon-filled lamps in respect of supply voltage, high ambient temperature, and humidity. There is a tighter restriction at low temperatures. Krypton-filled lamps should not be used below freezing, because of the effect of low temperatures on startability and light output.

4. On What Ballasts are they Suitable?

Krypton-filled lamps are for use on the Switch Start ballasts for the corresponding length argon-filled lamps. For example, the 58W 1500 mm (5 ft) lamp is operated on the 65W ballast for the 65/80W 1500 mm (5 ft) lamp. It then takes 58 Watts, whereas the 65/80W lamp takes 65 Watts.

Note: The 58W lamp must not be used on an 80W ballast.
    80W luminaires are obsolete and should be changed.
    Similarly the 70W lamp must not be used on an 85W ballast.

5. What Happens to Circuit Power?

This is reduced by the same amount as lamp power. For example, 65 lamp Watts plus 12 ballast Watts becomes 58 lamp Watts plus 12 ballast Watts. The saving is 7 Watts from 77, approximately 9 per cent. The same percentage applies to the saving in energy (kWh).

6. What Happens to Circuit Current and Power Factor (PF)?

The circuit current and hence the circuit VA stay the same, e.g. when a 58W lamp is operated on a 65W ballast. There is therefore no change required to ratings of cable, fuses, or circuit-breakers. Circuit Power Factor (W/VA) goes down by the same percentage as the circuit power. No change is required to PF capacitors in existing luminaires.

7. What Difference is there in Light Output?

The light output of a 26 mm diameter Krypton-filled lamp (e.g. 58W) is approximately the same as that of the higher rated 38 mm diameter argon-filled lamp (e.g. 65W).

Triphosphor krypton-filled lamps have approximately 10 per cent higher light output than the standard 38 mm diameter argon-filled lamps and approximately 70 per cent higher light output than 38 mm diameter argon-filled de-luxe lamps.

Table 7.8: Interchangeability of Lamps (Cont)

Tubular Fluorescent Lamps (Cont)

8. What is the Effect on Lighting Calculations?

For most luminaires, especially multi-lamp luminaires, the Light Output Ratio (LOR) is likely to be higher with 26 mm diameter lamps. The luminance of bare battens will be increased with 26 mm diameter lamps: but, with attachments such as diffusers, glare calculations should not be affected.

Discharge Lamps

The following notes provide outline guidance on the interchangeability of corresponding Discharge Lamps made by different lamp-makers who are LIF Members. The notes deal only with electrical interchangeability, and apply only where the control gear, especially the ballasts and ignitors, are made by LIF Members. Users should also check mechanical compatibility (e.g. the caps of double-ended linear high pressure sodium lamps).

High Pressure Mercury Lamps

Almost all of these lamps and their ballasts are covered by British Standards or IEC Specifications, and corresponding lamps are electrically interchangeable.

Note: Care should be taken to distinguish between the High Voltage and the Low Voltage versions of the MBF 1000W lamp.

Metal Halide Lamps

Different lamp-makers use different mixtures of halides, and the lamps are not interchangeable. A Metal Halide lamp must only be used on control gear as indicated by the lamp-maker.

Low Pressure Sodium Lamps

Almost all these lamps and their control gear (of conventional type) are covered by British Standards or IEC Specifications, and corresponding lamps are electrically interchangeable. This is also likely to apply where lamps are operated on partly-electronic ('hybrid') control gear made by LIF Members.

Note: For SLI lamps reference should be made to the data-sheets of the lamp makers.

High Pressure Sodium Lamps

The principal ratings and their control gear are covered by specifications, or are in draft specifications. Corresponding lamps of different makes are electrically interchangeable, but are of two types according to method of starting; lamps with an internal starting device are used on circuits without an ignitor; lamps without internal starting device are used on circuits which include an ignitor.

Note: Care should be taken to distinguish between the High Voltage and the Low Voltage versions of the 1000W lamp.

Plug-in HPS Lamps

These lamps are for replacing High Pressure Mercury lamps on ballasts which comply with specifications. Small changes may be required to ballast tapping, to values of PF capacitor, or to some wiring; reference should be made to the data-sheets of the lamp-makers.

Source: Lighting Industry Federation

available with external or internal ignitors and other types which are called 'plug in' HPS in as much as basically designed to operate on the same ballasts as the mercury lamps they can replace. Manufacturers would need to be consulted on suitability of existing circuit, as Table 7.8 indicates.

Costing Replacement Lighting

Table 7.9 sets out a framework for costing replacement lighting, in this case a change to high pressure sodium lamps but the approach adopted, and described in the following case study, can also be used for examining the cost benefits of moving to other types of lamp.

The case study involves an engineering workshop using 108–250 watt MBF/U industrial fittings to give an average lighting level of 500 lux. The same lighting level could be achieved from 54–250 watt HPS lamps in high bay fittings. The change to HPS would reduce electrical load, the number of points to maintain and the number of lamps to replace. But is the change worthwhile from a cost point of view?

In order to determine this—in terms of a straightforward payback analysis—some basic facts need to be established.

Burning Hours per Annum. This was established at 4,000 hours based on 16 hours per day, 5 days per week and 50 weeks per year.

Total Kilowatt Load. This is based on total circuit watts which are higher than discharge lamp wattage ratings.

Electricity Cost per Annum. Calculated on the basis of 2.2 pence per kilowatt hour inclusive of maximum demand and standing charges.

Cost of Replacement Lamps. The figure was based on nett trade prices.

Life of Replacement Lamps. This example assumes two years per lamp so that the accounting incorporates a 50 per cent replacement each year.

Labour Cost of Replacement Lamps. £2.50 per lamp has been taken as a nominal figure in this case. Many situations involve production shut downs or working outside normal hours.

Armed with this information a simple cost comparison between the existing and proposed lighting systems can be made. It is given in Table 7.10 and shows that the cost of the fittings will be recovered in well under three years.

Whilst this comparison does not incorporate all the cost factors it does illustrate clearly the importance of the running costs and particularly the cost of electricity. To continue to operate the existing lighting for a further ten years will cost over £27,000 (at today's fuel prices) whilst changing to high pressure sodium will bring a saving of £14,000 on the same basis. Within this context the cost of the new luminaires, at less than £3,000, appears modest and these calculations do not take account of future increases in fuel costs.

Luminaires

The energy-saving and economic advantages of using the most efficient lamp types suitable will be reduced or nullified if lamps are housed in inefficient luminaires.

The application efficiency of a luminaire relates to the efficiency of the luminaire in allowing the maximum proportion of the lamp light output to reach the working plane or surfaces being illuminated.

TABLE 7.9: COST COMPARISON FORM

Capital Costs	*Present Lighting*	*Proposed HP Sodium Lighting*
(a) Cost of Luminaires		_____ (Insert nett cost new fittings)

Running Costs

(b) Burning hours per annum	_____	_____
(c) Total kilowatt load	_____	_____
(d) Electricity cost per annum $$\frac{(p/kwH \times (b) \times (c))}{100}$$	_____	_____
(e) Cost of replacement lamps per annum $$\frac{(\text{cost per lamp} \times \text{number of lamps} \times (b))}{\text{estimated lamp life}}$$	_____	_____
(f) Labour cost of replacement lamps $$\frac{(\text{cost per lampway} \times \text{number of lamps} \times (b))}{\text{estimated lamp life}}$$	_____	_____
(g) **Annual Running Cost** (d+e+f)	_____	_____

High Pressure Sodium pay-back period =   _____years

$$\frac{(a)\ HPS}{(g)\ Present-(g)\ HPS}$$

Notes:

TABLE 7.10: A CASE STUDY COSTING OF A CHANGE TO H.P.S. LIGHTING

Capital Costs	Present Lighting	Proposed H.P.S. Lighting
(a) Cost of Luminaires	—	£2,900.56
Running Costs		
(b) Burning hours per annum	4,000	4,000
(c) Total kilowatt load	31.00 kw	15.08 kw
(d) Electricity cost per annum	£2,728.00	£1,327.04
(e) Cost of replacement lamps	361.26	748.71
(f) Labour cost of replacement lamps	135.00	67.50
Annual Running Cost	**£3,224.26**	**£2,143.25**

$$\text{High Pressure Sodium pay-back period} = \frac{£2,900.56}{£3,224.26 - £2,143.25} = 2.7 \text{ years}$$

The LOR (light output ratio) of a luminaire is not, in itself, a measurement of this efficiency; for example, a bare fluorescent tube in a batten type luminaire emits light in almost every direction and has a high LOR but more light will reach the working plane, say beneath the luminaire, if a suitable reflector is fitted to re-direct some of the light even though the LOR is reduced.

The most efficient luminaires are those which maximise the lighting result by the most suitable combination of light distribution and LOR. The only relevant method of assessment when lighting a horizontal working plane is to compare the UF's (utilization factors) of luminaires in each situation.

Determining the most efficient luminaires for lighting working planes which are vertical, or any angle other than horizontal, is more complex and it may be preferable to seek expert advice.

Other important considerations when choosing luminaires relate to maintenance. How easily can dirt and dust reduce the luminaire efficiency? Will any reflective surfaces or transmissive materials (prismatic controllers etc.) deteriorate permanently so that cleaning will not restore the performance?

Maintenance

Regular cleaning of lamps, luminaires and the interior room surfaces, where applicable, is essential if the lighting standards required, and designed for, are to be maintained.

Any circumstances which reduce the light output whilst the energy consumption and cost remains constant is a situation to be avoided.

Part of the maintenance programme for a lighting installation obviously includes changing the lamps. The light output of all lamps decreases during the operational life of the lamps, the rate of reduction depending upon the type of lamp.

Economic considerations generally dictate that the best results are achieved when lamps are replaced as a group, at the end of their economic service period, so minimising the labour costs involved—especially when lamp replacement is combined with cleaning of the luminaires.

Comprehensive information on this subject is provided in CIBS' Technical Report No. 9— 'Depreciation and Maintenance of Interior Lighting'.

FIGURE 7.11: LIGHTING CONTROL METHODS

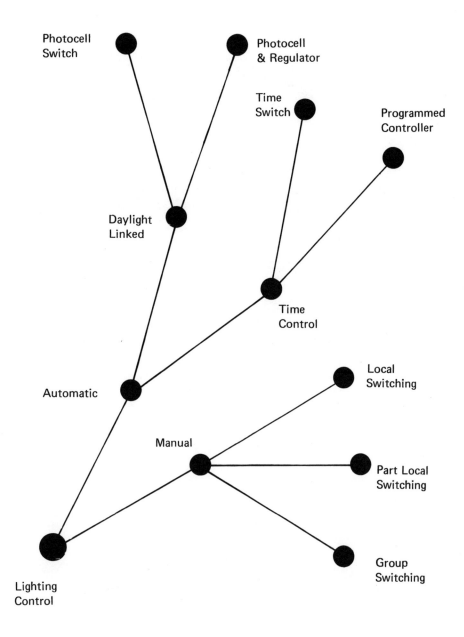

Controls

Lighting controls, whether automatic, semi automatic or manual, should ensure that:

  —sufficient lighting is provided when and where it is required and

  —lighting should be reduced or switched off whenever and wherever it is appropriate to do so.

The principal opportunities for reducing energy consumption of lighting by controls without any major risk of providing insufficient or unsuitable lighting are two-fold. The first is to control the main general lighting in the premises so that it is on or available only during the hours that the premises are occupied. Secondly, to use photo-cell controlled switching or regulation of the electric lighting in those zones which receive more than sufficient natural light during part of the occupied period.

Switch-off only types of controls result in a risk that the lighting provided is frequently insufficient and unsuitable and, as such, may reduce productivity.

A summary of lighting control types appears in Figure 7.11.

Design

Much can be done in the overall design to avoid the waste of light and therefore energy. Lighting installations are frequently designed on the assumption that the total area contains little or no obstruction to the flow of light. Often, such as in open-plan offices with relatively low furniture, it is correct to do so but in some instances, e.g. production areas with tall machinery, this approach may lead to screening of luminaires resulting in poor utilisation, energy waste and probably insufficient light on the visual task.

There is little point in designing the lighting of a total area, in which there are various visual tasks, to provide the highest illuminance required. If flexibility within the total area is a requirement, use multi-lamp luminaires so that they can be controlled to use less lamps in those areas requiring lower illuminances.

Conclusions

Whilst the need to conserve energy, and so minimise lighting costs, when designing new lighting installations is obvious, the greatest potential for energy cost saving in lighting lies in those many existing lighting installations which need converting to use modern, more efficient lamps, luminaires and so on.

Whether converting an existing, or designing a new, lighting installation the achievement of sufficient and suitable standards of lighting is essential if the overall energy and cost management objectives are to be fulfilled.

Useful References

CIBS Code for Interior Lighting, Chartered Institution of Building Services.
CIBS Technical Report No. 9, Chartered Institution of Building Services.
LIF Factfinder No.3—Lamp Guide, Lighting Industry Federation.
LIF Factfinder No.4—Lighting and Energy, Lighting Industry Federation.

8

TRANSPORT AND GARAGE MANAGEMENT

Bill Kirkland

This chapter concentrates on those aspects of energy management of specific relevance to the operation of vehicles and garage premises. The examples given, coming from the author's personal experience, refer to the operation of commercial passenger vehicles although the principles and practice involved generally have much wider application. Premises are dealt with first including a detailed account of the recent installation of an energy recovery wheel at a garage. Aspects of energy efficient vehicle operation are then discussed and the chapter concludes with a review of developments in vehicle design.

Energy-Saving in Depots and Garages

There are essentially three ways of conserving energy in these premises:-

—by not doing things e.g. by not heating parking areas energy can be conserved

—by doing things to a reduced standard e.g. by reducing temperature settings in a heated area to the lowest acceptable level

—by doing things as before but using less energy.

The first two options attack the established comfort standards in the working environment and, as such, are likely to meet stiff resistance from employees. They are not therefore widely acceptable measures. Unless considerable savings can be achieved, or unless previous practice has been out of line with general standards, they are probably not worthy of special attention at an early stage in the energy conservation programme.

It is the third option, therefore, which generally demands attention, offering considerable potential to reduce energy consumption without attacking comfort standards.

But before exploring this option there is an interesting example of how investigating and changing previous practice can lead to substantial energy savings at low cost. When people start on the heat economy trail they frequently think in either high technology terms or simple administrative procedures aimed, for example, at switching out all the lights or keeping the heater thermostat low. Both of these have their role to play, but relatively low cost, low level technology installations and rearrangements should not be overlooked. They too, can bring energy and consequently cost savings.

A clear example was found at the Central Works of the South Yorkshire Passenger Transport Executive (SYPTE). The main entrance to the works is 32 feet high and 16 feet wide. It leads into the main body of the works and from there out onto a bus park at the rear of the premises.

In a recent survey it was found that buses use the entrance on average only 12 times per day, whereas staff cars and motorcycles, light vans and small lorries use the entrance a total of 106 times a day. Virtually all the traffic was merely passing through to the bus park at the rear which involved travelling through the covered area and out through another smaller door at the rear to the outside. Measurements of heat loss revealed that with an ambient temperature of 8°C, the internal temperature dropped by 2°C during the opening and closing cycle of the door.

The solution did not involve any high cost technology, and was simply one of common sense. A small piece of land adjacent to the works was purchased when it became available, and a new entrance was constructed which did not pass through any of the buildings. Once commissioned, only buses have been allowed to use the old entrance, and although the savings are difficult to estimate, with a winter fuel bill for these premises averaging £2,450 per week and with a 32 feet by 16 feet hole not opening and closing 3½ hours per day, it is confidently expected that substantial savings will be made.

In order to ensure that labour costs did not run away with the energy savings, remote controls were fitted to the original entrance door with a television and voice system allowing the doorman at the new entrance to control both doors from the one spot. Apart from the energy savings there is now a one-way system and better security to the premises. It is expected that the cost will be paid for within one to two years from the energy savings alone.

Similar opportunities exist within other SYPTE premises and a number are under investigation. They offer the prospect of energy savings in a controlled manner but without the use of high technology.

The SYPTE has taken a three-fold approach to promoting energy conservation measures in their premises, namely

—encouraging good housekeeping and staff motivation
—examining building services and plant and
—uprating building fabric.

Good Housekeeping and Staff Motivation

Diligence in the use of energy, and an awareness of the costs involved, help to develop good habits among employees to avoid the unnecessary use of building services and equipment. The role of local supervision is critical to the irresponse. The workforce cannot be expected to respond to a call for economy from a supervisor who operates from an overheated office and leaves the lights switched on.

Spot checks will frequently discover that the automatic control system has been placed on manual override. The supervisor must exercise proper control and discipline over employees who habitually waste energy and he must be supported by senior management. Failure in this critical area will lead to bad housekeeping being tolerated, and much energy waste.

Responsibility for managing energy costs must be apportioned and allocated to those who are able to exercise control over utilisation. How often is responsibility for management of energy costs expressed as a specific responsibility on job descriptions?

A wide range of techniques and methods are available to managers in their efforts to motivate employees towards the achievement of specific goals, and these techniques are increasingly being applied to energy conservation. For example, some companies have developed an MBO (management by objectives) scheme by identifying key people who have control over energy utilisation, and setting targets for them to achieve. Another approach has been the application of the concept of 'quality circles' to involve employees in solving energy conservation problems. This is a 'bottoms-up' approach to the management of energy costs involving the devolution of some decision making power to the 'quality circle' and the group leader. To be successful it requires the commitment of top management and an education programme for those inolved in working in groups.

A growing range of films and publicity material is available which enables companies to embark upon campaigns. It is suggested that selective topics or themes are taken in turn as the subject of a campaign, and repeated at appropriate intervals to communicate with employees. This technique is probably more suitable for the larger companies.

Suggestion schemes can be operated in which employees are offered rewards for making suggestions which lead to a reduction in energy consumption. Whatever the technique employed, the aim must be to secure employee participation in the energy conservation programme.

Building Services and Plant

Heating and ventilation systems should be checked to ensure that the garage is not overheated and that they are not operating when the building, or parts of the building, are unoccupied. Energy recovery is also an option. One system has been installed with good results at a garage and a second is in the process of installation at another. The system is based on the energy recovery wheel and has been applied to an integrated heating and ventilation system. Subsequent monitoring of performance has indicated an average energy recovery efficiency of 75 per cent, thus confirming the anticipated cost benefits. A full account of this particular project is given in a later section of this chapter.

Check the usage of lighting and power. Are lights and machines left running when not in use? Many examples are to be found where comparatively low technology has been used to control heating, lighting and power. For example, the use of a simple induction loop has enabled previously motorised doors to be opened and closed automatically when approached by buses. Similarly lighting levels have been improved at low cost by replacing old fluorescent systems with high pressure sodium light fittings. The energy conservation package has been completed by applying a combination of timers and solar control devices to ensure that even the more economical sodium lighting is not left on when it is not needed.

The installation of power factor correction equipment in SYPTE depots has proved extremely attractive financially: the pay back on one recent example being measured in months rather than years. (For a general description on power factor correction see page 13.)

Furthermore the rapid development of micro-computer technology has made it possible to fully automate the control of heating, lighting and ventilation systems, and virtually every kind of workshop equipment having a regular usage pattern i.e. compressors, refrigerators, process heaters, etc. Apart from interfacing with system controls, the micro-computer provides other benefits in terms of a comprehensive, quicker, and less time consuming energy monitoring and targeting system. The micro-computer itself is comparatively cheap, but the interfacing with existing system controls, or in some cases the installation of new system controls, can be expensive. Each application must be subjected to cost effective evaluation.

SYPTE engineers are currently investigating the use of an energy management system in garages and early indications are that the system can offer an economical way to *control costs*, and at the same time reduce the *exposure risk to uncontrolled increases in costs*. Initially the system would be designed to interface with existing traditional control equipment and services for heating, lighting, domestic hot water, compressors, boilers, and associated equipment. In the long term the system would be used to monitor and record total energy utilisation, including diesel fuel. The central micro-computer has the capacity to receive additional garages at a future date and, as a bonus, it may also be used as a maintenance tool, capable of monitoring usage, indicating when maintenance of services and equipment is due, and storing the maintenance schedules.

The Building Fabric

Scope to improve the performance of the building fabric has also been found, particularly in older property, by the application of thermal insulation to walls and roofs. The financial viability of such measures can be improved if insulation can be incorporated into re-roofing for maintenance reasons. Often in more modern property insulation has only been found to be viable when coupled with maintenance work in this way.

A range of other measures is possible, e.g. insulated false ceilings, double glazing, and solar film. Glazing heat losses have been found particularly difficult to deal with. The high cost of double glazing is often prohibitive, and whilst the application of 'factory liner' is more likely to be viable, the effect in loss of natural light has to be taken into consideration.

Implementing a Practical Policy for Energy-Saving

It is vital at the outset to ensure that the selection of energy conservation measures is made on a commercial basis. For example, during a recent energy survey at one of SYPTE's premises, some 45 ways of conserving energy were identified, but after more detailed investigation and cost evaluation, only 15 were found to be economically viable. Many of the remaining 30 items would have been viable for incorporation into a new construction or project, but the cost of modifying existing property and systems was found to be prohibitive. Others were simply not satisfactory financial propositions.

Implementation of policy requires a plan for action; an 'energy management programme'. One of the fundamental parts of all successful energy management programmes is an energy monitoring and targeting system. Identification of where the energy goes, and regular monitoring of usage is basic information needed to plan and control conservation programmes. The information is also essential in preparing the 'energy budget'. There is a need to monitor energy on a regular basis and allow targets to be identified. Energy utilisation efficiency can then be assessed and specific areas of consumption identified and reduced to a programmed schedule.

The next step is to examine the nature of energy consumption, which requires an understanding of the engineering process of energy consumption. Without this the interpretation of the output from the energy monitoring system will be lacking, and the system may do little more than summarise consumptions. The energy consultant has a role to play in surveying premises and identifying property, building services and equipment which have low energy efficiency, and by investigating ways of improving the situation. The term 'consultant' is linked by many people with high fees. There is a need to ensure that the consultant's efforts are concentrated into the areas offering the greatest benefits. This has been done in the SYPTE by splitting the energy survey into three parts:-

Stage 1 - An initial broad brush survey to identify potential energy saving measures.

Stage 2 - After careful vetting of these by the Executive an agreement is reached with the consultant to carry out a detailed investigation and cost benefit analysis of the promising measures only.

Stage 3 - Implementation of those measures approved under Stage 2 as being cost effective.

Under the current economic environment lack of finance is likely to crop up as the principal problem in implementing an energy-saving policy. Energy conservation measures are normally only accepted on the basis of being cost effective. Measures proposed have to be very attractive in offering substantial early savings. In the survey referred to earlier, the 15 measures accepted for implementation were cost effective within two years on a simple pay back method. An alternative approach where measures are suitable for leasing finance is to compare the annual lease charges with the annual savings. The capital cost of implementing the 15 measures was £30,000, equating to an annual leasing charge of approximately £7,200 (over five years) which is then compared with annual savings of almost £18,000. Obviously, this equation becomes more or less attractive, depending on the period of amortisation of the investment.

Apart from the cost of capital and the amortisation period, the other major factor is the rate of inflation, and how this will affect the future cost of energy. There are a number of more sophisticated capital investment appraisal techniques to cope with this problem, e.g. the internal rate of return method, and these are discussed in Chapter 3.

Heat Recovery in Garage Premises

The introduction of a heat recovery wheel by the SYPTE at one of its garages is a good example of a successful energy-saving project in the transport sector.

High levels of ventilation are needed in garages to comply with the Health and Safety legislation. Without some form of energy recovery heat loss is considerable. And in this particular case high running costs would have been added to by the requirement for increased boiler plant and an additional building to house the equipment.

Consequently, an early decision was taken to investigate the known forms of energy recovery devices, and assess both their suitability and viability for the bus garage application. There are several devices which could have done the job, but it soon became apparent that the energy recovery wheel was going to be more economically viable.

The Energy Recovery Wheel

The energy recovery wheel is a rotary air-to-air energy exchanger which is installed between the exhaust and supply air ductwork in a heating, ventilating, or air conditioning system. It is capable of recovering a large proportion of the total energy from the exhaust air stream before it is exhausted to atmosphere, and transfers this energy to the incoming fresh air supply. Considerable benefits can be obtained in terms of both reductions in running costs and the reduction in the size and cost of the heating and/or cooling plant. The energy exchanger matrix comprises a permanent transfer medium which is lightweight, inert, and operates with the moisture content of the air remaining in the vapour state. This keeps the matrix dry, reduces the possibility of bacteria or algae growth, and makes it suitable for recovery of both sensible and latent heat. An efficiency of over 70 per cent can be obtained. The matrix is rotated at a speed of approximately 10 rpm, thus having a very low power requirement and long life. As the exhaust air stream passes through the matrix of the rotating exchanger wheel, a proportion of the air will become entrained within the matrix, and due to the wheel's rotation will be carried towards the incoming fresh air stream. The transfer of insoluble airborne odours or particles between the air flows is prevented by a *purge sector* in the wheel which reduces carry over to less than 0.04 per cent by volume.

The heat wheel can be incorporated into many types of new or existing heating and ventilating systems in a wide variety of buildings. However, its application to the recovery of energy in a bus garage presented particular problems because of the dual requirement to remove toxic fumes from the environment and make savings in running costs.

Testing Suitability

The decision to install the heat wheel was taken on purely commercial grounds. The initial survey took into consideration the additional capital cost of installing the necessary equipment, together with the projected savings in running costs to ascertain the economic viability of the system. Having confirmed the commercial benefits, the problem of introducing the heat wheel into an environment of toxic fumes was assessed. Whilst manufacturers gave assurances that toxic fume carry over would not be a problem, and references were made to installations involving similar environments in Europe, independent tests could not be produced, and there were no UK installations which demonstrated satisfactory operation in similar application. Consequently, with assistance from the manufacturer, a sample heat wheel was installed for the purpose of carrying out independent tests under the scrutiny of the local Factory Inspectorate.

The testing was assembled to allow exhaust fumes from two bus engines to be ducted through one half of the wheel to outside, and fresh air to be brought through the other half of the wheel into the garage. The exhaust air discharge *outlet* and fresh air *input* were tested with instrumentation employing *Drager tubes*, to assess the levels of gases, and make a comparison.

The tests carried out measured the levels of carbon monoxide, sulphur dioxide, and oxides of nitrogen. The results indicated no discernible carry over of sulphur dioxide and oxides of nitrogen, and a carry over of 5 ppm (parts per million) of carbon monoxide. It was concluded that this was well within present and possible future threshold limit values and would not cause any build up of fumes. The decision was confirmed therefore to install heat wheels.

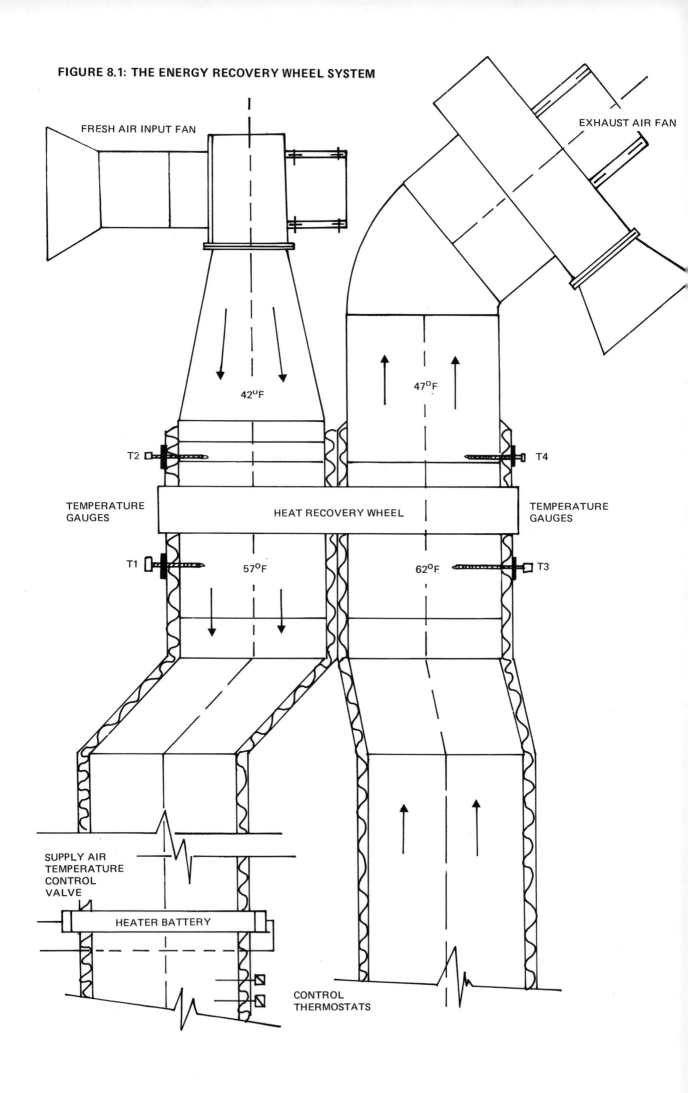

FIGURE 8.1: THE ENERGY RECOVERY WHEEL SYSTEM

FRESH AIR INPUT FAN

EXHAUST AIR FAN

42°F

47°F

T2

T4

TEMPERATURE
GAUGES

HEAT RECOVERY WHEEL

TEMPERATURE
GAUGES

T1

57°F

62°F

T3

SUPPLY AIR
TEMPERATURE
CONTROL
VALVE

HEATER BATTERY

CONTROL
THERMOSTATS

System Design

The system, as designed, is made up of three elements:

  —the heating element,
  —the ventilating element, and
  —the energy recovery element.

The design consists of ducted extract and supply air systems to the parking areas and workshops, the extraction route having been designed to reduce the level of toxic fumes to at least 50 per cent of the TLV (threshold limit value), thus allowing a comfortable margin for safety. This equated to approximately 3½ air changes per hour. The supply and extract ducts are so positioned as to run through the heat wheel.

A further design consideration was the spatial requirements of the system and the need to avoid loss of valuable vehicle parking and workshop space. This led to the decision to install the plant on the roof of the building. The system controls were fully automated and located in the supervisor's office—to avoid unauthorised tampering with controls.

Operating Experiences

During the first heating season the system was closely monitored to check the efficiency and observe for potential maintenance problems. Graph temperature recorders were located in the duct work, and the results logged monthly. A physical inspection of random wheels was also carried out at monthly intervals.

A plan of the ventilation plant arrangement is given in Figure 8.1 and the test results and calculations of cost savings are shown in Table 8.2. The results indicate an average efficiency across ten heat wheels of 75 per cent, confirming that the anticipated reductions in running costs were actually achieved. However, the incorporation of heat wheels provides an added air resistance to the ventilation system and a consequent increase in fan power is necessary. When determining the actual fuel savings therefore, the additional cost of electricity must be taken into consideration.

Measurement of air resistance across the heat wheel indicates that the additional cost of electricity can be as high as 25 per cent of the total cost of the power requirements of the ventilation system. A visual inspection of the wheel after twelve months operation indicated minor traces of oil deposits on the face of the wheel, but these were not found to be detrimental to performance. Annual cleaning of the wheels has been found to be adequate in spite of the decision *not* to incorporate filters in the ductwork. However, this would become a necessity if it was decided to connect vehicle exhaust pipes direct into the system. The cores of the wheels were found generally to be free of dust and other contaminants, with only a bucket full of dirt being removed from all ten wheels after a full twelve months operation.

The indications are that the manufacturer's claim that the wheels are 'self cleaning' is not unreasonable, and it may be concluded that the device is suitable for industrial environments.

The garage is located very close to a housing estate and in consequence noise was a potential problem. Substantial air intake silencers were fitted and there have been no complaints from residents in over three years.

Conclusion

The use of the heat wheel in bus garages has been found to be commercially viable, and the equipment both reliable and requiring minimal maintenance. Notwithstanding this success however, it should not be presumed that heat wheels would necessarily be equally successful in all bus garages. It is not a panacea for energy recovery problems. For example, studies to apply the heat wheel to an *existing* ventilation system have indicated that the costs are prohibitive. The physical requirements of the device may also present difficulties. The main reasons for the economical viability of energy recovery wheels in the SYPTE's garage were:-

TABLE 8.2: TEST RESULTS AND CALCULATIONS OF COST SAVINGS OF HEAT RECOVERY SYSTEM

The general arrangement of the ventilation systems incorporating the heat wheels is as shown in Figure 8.1. Temperature gauges have been incorporated at the points shown and typical readings obtained are indicated on the diagram.

From these figures the efficiency of heat recovery for equal air volumes on supply and exhaust can be calculated as follows:-

$$\text{Efficiency of Heat Recovery} = \frac{T_2 - T_1}{T_3 - T_1} \times 100 \text{ per cent}$$

Where:

$-T_1$ is the temperature of extract air drawn through the wheel
$-T_2$ is the temperature of the supply air after passing over the wheel
$-T_3$ is the temperature of the exhaust air from the building.

For the temperatures shown on Figure 8.1 the efficiency is:-

$$\frac{57-42}{62-42} \times 100 = \frac{15}{20} \times 100 = 75 \text{ per cent}$$

Similar readings have been taken for each of the ten wheels over a period of three months and a summary of the temperatures obtained at different ambient conditions and calculated efficiencies are as follows:-

Fan Station Number	Air Temperatures of:				Efficiency of Heat Recovery (Per Cent)
	Outside Ambient	Supply Air to Garage	Exhaust Air from Garage	Exhaust Air from Wheel	
	T1	T2	T3	T4	
1	42	57	62	47	75
2	55	60	63	57	63
3	34	56	62	42	79
4	46	59	63	49	77
5	37	53	61	43	67
6	52	61	63	55	82
7	40	57	62	48	77
8	45	59	63	49	78
9	52	59	62	54	70
10	59	64	65	60	83

The average efficiency of the above figure is 75 per cent.

The difference in efficiencies for each wheel can be attributed to the accuracy of the instrumentation used and differing air volumes on supply and extract fans. Higher efficiencies would occur where the exhaust air volume exceeds the supply air volume and low efficiencies where the supply air volume exceeds the exhaust air volume. The ventilation systems operate in one large area and minor differences in volumes of air exhausted and supplied averages out as the overall efficiency attained indicates.

Table 8.2: Test Results and Calculations of Cost Savings of Heat Recovery System (Cont)

From the efficiencies calculated the fuel costs savings can be determined as follows:-

TOTAL HEAT REQUIREMENTS OF VENTILATION SYSTEM

Ambient Air Temperature	60°F
Outside Air Temperature	30°F
Total Air Volume	120,00 cfm
Specific Heat of Air	0.02 Btus/ft^3 $^\circ$F
Total Heat Input	= 120.000 x 30 x 0.02 x 60
	= 4,320.000 Btus/hour

OPERATING HOURS

Plant Operating Periods	0600–0800 and 1500–1700 hours
Total Hours	= 4 per day
Total Annual Hours	= 4 x 7 x 52
	= 1,456

Assuming a weather factor of 0.5 for the Doncaster Area

Total Annual Operating Hours at Maximum Demand = 728

FUEL COSTS

(i) GAS

Total Annual Heat Requirements $= \dfrac{4,320,000 \times 728}{100,000}$

= 31,450 therms of heat

With an efficiency of Heat Recovery of 75 per cent the saving on heat input from the gas fired boiler plant would be:-

31,450 x 0.75 = 23,587 therms

For a boiler plant combustion efficiency of 75 per cent and gas at 31.3 pence per therm

Annual Gas Cost $= \dfrac{23,587 \times 31.3}{0.75 \quad 100}$

= £9,843.00

(ii) ELECTRICITY

Additional Power Requirements = 30 kVA

Additional Fuel Consumption = 42,000 units

Cost of electricity at £20 per kVA and 3.0 pence per unit

$= 20 \times 30 \times 42,000 \times \dfrac{3}{100}$

= £1,860.00

(iii) NET FUEL SAVING = £9,843–£1,860

= £7,983 per annum

—the wheels were incorporated into a *new* input/extract ventilation scheme, and consequently the associated ductwork was designed to accommodate the wheel in the most economical manner possible, and

—the building construction offered a flat roof which allowed the siting of the relatively heavy heat wheels with minimal structural support.

Energy Saving in Vehicle Operation

These principal areas identified by SYPTE for improving fleet operating efficiency are now summarised together with a review of the measures taken so far. Actions which can be taken immediately or within a short period of time and without involving any great expense are described first.

Correct Driver Training

Correct driver training, if effectively carried out, can save the average operator somewhere between two and five per cent of fuel costs. Driver training covers several areas which could be attributed as fuel saving areas, notably the correct use of the gears and the throttle system. The SYPTE trains drivers on both the semi-automatic type transmission as well as the fully automatic system. The semi-automatic system is designed so that the driver changes gear by the use of an electrical switch, the change in the gearbox being carried out by air pressure. This type of system allows the driver to select whichever gear he thinks appropriate but, although very flexible in its approach, is also subject to abuse by the untrained or ill-informed driver. Holding on to a low gear or changing up into a higher gear can severely affect the fuel efficiency of the engine and can result in damage such as propshaft and axle overstressing which can be the cause of severe vehicle breakdowns.

But with current day traffic flows the standard approach now being adopted is to use only fully automatic gearboxes. Fully automatics allow the driver to hold gears when necessary for hill-climbing but do not allow the gear to be held on the flat or on downhill stretches where damage to the transmission could occur. Also the electronic control unit which controls these automatic boxes, keeps the vehicle in the correct gear at all times depending on the position of the throttle pedal and the fuel rack on the engine, thus ensuring the most fuel efficient operation of the engine.

The correct control of the vehicle's speed can also save a large amount of fuel as excess speed coming into traffic stops or standard bus stops and the use of severe braking not only causes strain on the vehicle and the passengers but wastes fuel. Again, correct driver training can ensure that the vehicle and the passengers have a smooth ride and fuel is saved.

Ensuring Engines are not Running Unnecessarily

This primarily means shutting down the engine when it is not required for moving the vehicle, mainly at termini or at bus stations and during maintenance. In normal operations the work cycle of a bus engine is 55 per cent of the time on idling, the other 45 per cent of the time spent at engine speeds between maximum and idling. But the actual time spent on maximum is as low as five per cent. Obviously the 55 per cent of the time on idling is not all at termini or in garages but during the normal running of the vehicle at traffic stops, bus stops, etc., when, with existing technology, it would be uneconomical to stop the engine.

Reducing Losses during Refuelling

Losses during refuelling can be split mainly into two areas: accidental fuel spillage and pilfering of fuel. The accidental spillage of fuel is by far and away the greatest wastage of fuel in public service undertakings, although the amount of fuel lost during refuelling can be reduced by as much as 75 per cent by the fitting of automatic shut down nozzles on the fuelling system. These nozzles are basically the same as those used in self-service petrol stations and stop the flow of fuel when a back pressure is detected.

The design of the fuel tank can also reduce fuel spillage quite dramatically. The tanks specified by SYPTE are fitted with a large diameter fuel neck. This together with high volume low pressure fuelling pumps reduce the foaming of the fuel in the bus tank and allow the tank to be filled to capacity without causing a backflow of fuel from the fuel neck as shown in Figure 8.3.

Losses due to pilfering can be controlled by the use of microprocessor control fuel pumps. A new garage under construction in Rotherham District starting this year will be fitted with fuel pumps to this design which require a security key and a valid bus number punched into the micro-computer before fuel can be supplied. A printed read-out from this pump allows fuel taken, security key code number, and bus number all to be inputed directly into the main frame computer. This not only provides secure refuelling but allows fuelling data to be inputed directly with consequential manpower savings.

Improved Maintenance to Reduce Fuel Wastage

Lack of regular maintenance to items such as the fuel injector pump and fuel injectors can detrimentally affect fuel consumption by as much as eight per cent. These should be overhauled at twelve month intervals using fuel test rigs as shown in Table 8.4. This eliminates fuel wastage which comes mainly from the lack of power from the engine due to poor fuel metering and/or poor injection necessitating the driver to be heavy footed with the throttle to maintain the same running times. Incorrect engine timing is also a major contributory factor to poor engine perform-ance and should also be reset regularly.

Road Testing

It is normal practice within bus operations, to road test the vehicle after some minor alterations or repairs. This, even in a well organised operation can mean a road test of some five miles per vehicle and could, in an operation the size of South Yorkshire, result in an annual wastage mileage of 120,000 miles. This mileage has been severely curtailed by the installation of brake testers and static test equipment. Brake testers can be used to check all work carried out on braking systems and do a far better checking test than a road test did in previous years. The use of static test equipment to plug into automatic transmissions which will carry out a full transmission check whilst the vehicle is stationary also serves to reduce fuel wastage.

Equipment for Improving Vehicle Performance

Radial-ply Tyres

The use of radial-ply tyres in the bus industry has, on average, reduced fuel consumption by 5½ to 8 per cent. This fuel saving over the normal old-fashioned type crossply tyres is primarily due to reduced rolling resistance due to the flexibility of the tyre sidewalls. In the old crossply tyres fuel was wasted by generating heat in the tyre carcase. This also caused degradation of the tyre build-up and in certain cases resulted in tyre failures. Radial-ply tyres therefore not only save fuel but also are of a safer construction.

FIGURE 8.3: HIGH VOLUME LOW PRESSURE FUEL PUMPS

FIGURE 8.4: FUEL TEST RIG

Engine Oils

The specification of engine oil used can have a marginal effect on the fuel consumption. A 15w 40 low ash multigrade engine oil has been used in the SYPTE area for the past three years. This engine oil gives a low 15w viscosity when the vehicle and temperatures are cold, thus reducing the cranking torque required by the starter motor and also the engine frictional losses at low temperatures, thereby saving fuel. The 40 grade viscosity when hot, gives better protection at the extremely high temperatures which can be found on rear engined vehicles. Multigrade lubricant not only saves energy directly as fuel but also reduces the repair costs and the downtime on the engine due to its improved lubrication.

Fuel Additives

There are arguments both for and against fuel additives which essentially add bulk to the fuel tank. Clearly if performance can be maintained when say an additive constituting ten per cent of the tank total is introduced then an improvement in fuel economy of up to ten per cent must have been achieved. The water injection system offered, also carries out a similar process to fuel additives. Water, of up to ten per cent in volume, is injected into the fuel, thus making up the bulk of the delivered fuel metered by the fuel pump.

Obviously the direct effect is that the engine itself delivers some ten per cent less power. If the operation of the vehicle can be satisfactorily run at this low power level a clear fuel saving will result. But if, as is found within South Yorkshire, the engine power and torque ratings are used to the full on many of our routes, the fuel saving envisaged is not recovered. Also if a ten per cent lower power rating can be accepted, it would be easier and cheaper to lower the power rating and thus the fuel delivery of the existing fuel pump.

Hydraulic Cooling Fan Systems

These systems use a hydraulic motor to drive the radiator cooling fan as against the previous system, driven mechanically directly off the engine. This allows the fan to be thermostatically controlled and does not waste any engine power whilst the cooling system is running up to operating temperature.

It has been proved within the SYPTE operations that with a front mounted radiator bus the fan only requires to run for some five minutes every 30 to 40 minutes depending on the ambient temperature. As the average fan on a double deck vehicle absorbs approximately five horsepower it is clear that reducing fan running time by the use of hydraulics will bring significant energy savings.

Obviously the improved warm-up time saves fuel by quickly reaching the maximum operating temperature. Maintaining this temperature can also have a small beneficial effect on fuel consumption. This leads into a second area, radiator shutters.

Radiator Shutters

These are air operated, thermostatically controlled and fitted immediately in front of the front radiator. They allow a quicker warm-up time and maintain a constant engine coolant temperature.

Without radiator shutters, a graph of engine temperature would show peaks and troughs throughout the normal operating cycle. These peaks and troughs not only affect the thermal efficiency of the engine but also give severe thermal shock to the engine components when cold water from the radiator system floods into an extremely hot engine.

With the radiator shutters in circuit, these various peaks and troughs are smoothed out to a mere ripple thus reducing thermal shocks and keeping the engine at a more satisfactory operating temperature throughout its life.

Future Developments

Automatic Engine Cut-Out

A system designed to cut out an engine when idling is now in use in Switzerland. The period the engine is allowed to remain idling will depend on the type of operation the vehicle is being used for but the SYPTE expects to set a time lapse of three to five seconds for the vehicle to idle before the engine is cut out. It involves the removal of the low pressure air system and the electrical starter motor from the vehicle and the substitution of a high pressure compressor and air system rated at approximately 600 p.s.i.

The engine itself is controlled via a microprocessor/timeswitch which senses when the engine is on idling and after a pre-determined time, which can be variously set, stops the diesel engine. This can happen in traffic or anywhere where the engine is idling longer than the specified time.

Obviously the driver is aware that the engine has stopped but he requires no further action than to press the accelerator when he requires to move forward. This action initiates the air distribution system mounted on the engine and the high pressure compressed air is fed directly into the cylinders via injection valves. The engine starts and goes on to power almost immediately. Tests carried out by the designers have shown that the engine will start within half a revolution and come onto normal power within two revolutions of the engine. The driver can detect no difference between this type of operation and a standard vehicle whilst the projected savings on shutting down the engine at intermediate traffic stops can be as much as ten per cent of the fuel.

Automatic Control Aids

Developments are in hand for the use of an on-board microprocessor to control the engine power setting and gear selection. This system removes from the driver the engine speed and power setting and also the control of the gearbox.

A microprocessor is positioned between the driving controls and the engine/transmission systems such that the driver can select one of three driving modes, these being economy, normal or express. This switch signals to the microprocessor the speed rating of the operation required. The throttle pedal also gives an input signal to the microprocessor, again indicating that the driver either requires more or less speed. The microprocessor then integrates the information from the input i.e. the three-position switch and the throttle pedal and selects the best possible gear and the correct engine speed to give optimum performance.

With this system, the diesel engine is always operating at its optimum level and the gears are selected to give optimum performance bearing in mind the speed requirements of the service set by the driver. It is envisaged that this type of system will be evolved in the next three to five years and indications are that fuel savings could be in the 10 to 15 per cent range.

Battery Powered Vehicles

Considerable development has been undertaken over the last five years on the development of a more energy dense battery than the standard lead-acid. These developments have included the zinc air and sodium sulphur batteries but, unfortunately in their scaled up version large enough to propel a large heavy goods or public service vehicle, the packages themselves have not proved very successful and future power sources involving batteries are still some ten years away.

Although lead-acid batteries do provide an efficient power source for small delivery vehicles, and maybe small public service vehicles, large vehicles have insufficient range or acceleration.

9

A PRACTICAL EXERCISE IN ENERGY AUDITING

David Yuill

As part of the session dealing with the energy survey, covered in Chapter 2, delegates to the National Energy Managers' Workshop carry out their own energy survey of their college buildings.

This Chapter contains the basic information supplied to the delegates on the fuel consumption and costs derived from prior metering and analysis. This is the type of information which an energy manager should be able to obtain on his own plant and premises without too much difficulty. Points highlighted for particular investigation by the session leader, David Yuill, an industrial energy consultant, are also referred to at this stage.

Mr Yuill's final report, based on his own one day survey, is then reproduced showing that sizable annual savings in fuel costs could be achieved with very little expenditure and even greater savings are available within a payback of two to three years. The report is presented to the structure laid down by the Department of Energy and is therefore illustrative of the type of approach that could be expected from a consultant hired under the one day Energy Survey Scheme.

The College Buildings

The original nineteenth century mansion has been extended in recent decades, as has the original stable block (known as the old quad), with modern kitchen, dining and residential accommodation. Annex A is the last remaining unit of several large huts of temporary standard. The layout of these buildings can be seen in the plan in Figure 9.1.

The total floor area of the mansion block is a little over 60,000 square feet with an additional 18,000 square feet in the two quads and Annex A. Room heights were taken as approximately 10 feet throughout.

The walls of both the old and new buildings in the mansion have only moderate U value ratings but improved insulation is considered unlikely to offer a good return. The concourse area contains large windows but these have already been double-glazed.

The new quad block being of recent construction is likewise expected to offer little prospect for additional cost-effective insulation. But the loft in the old quad has remained uninsulated giving a U value for the roof of 2.2 W/m^2 $^{\circ}C$. The introduction of mineral quilt insulation to a thickness of 100 mm would cost about £2.50 per square metre installed but would dramatically reduce the U value to the order of 0.3 W/m^2 $^{\circ}C$.

Likewise Annex A deserves attention: the double skin walls are uninsulated, as are the roof and floors. Glazing accounts for about 20 per cent of the wall area. The present and potential U values for this structure are given in Table 9.2.

Scope of the Survey

The energy survey would concentrate on the main heat and power requirements of the college namely the space heating and provision of hot water to the mansion, the two quads and Annex A. Heating of staff cottages, electricity for pumping the college water supply and cooking in the main kitchen by a separate LPG supply were to be excluded.

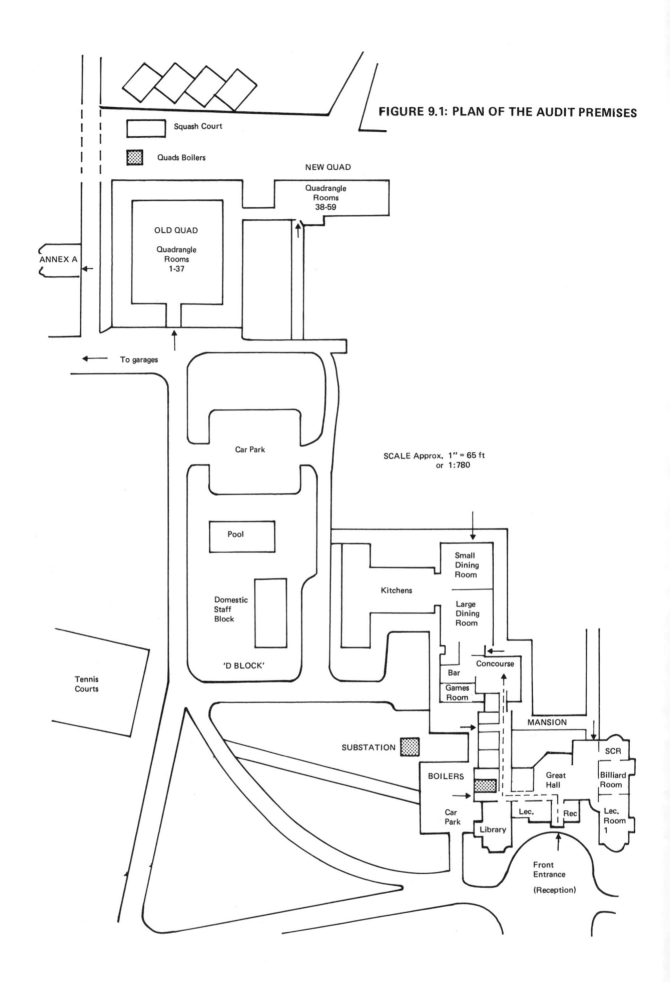

FIGURE 9.1: PLAN OF THE AUDIT PREMISES

Squash Court

Quads Boilers

NEW QUAD

Quadrangle
Rooms
38-59

OLD QUAD

Quadrangle
Rooms
1-37

ANNEX A

To garages

Car Park

SCALE Approx. 1″ = 65 ft
or 1:780

Pool

Small
Dining
Room

Kitchens

Large
Dining
Room

Domestic
Staff
Block

Concourse

Bar

Games
Room

'D BLOCK'

MANSION

Tennis
Courts

SUBSTATION

SCR

Billiard
Room

BOILERS

Great
Hall

Car
Park

Lec.

Rec

Lec.
Room
1

Library

Front
Entrance

(Reception)

TABLE 9.2: INSULATION DATA FOR ANNEX A

	Present U value W/m^2 $^\circ$C	Improved U value W/m^2 $^\circ$C	Budgeted Cost (£ per sq metre)	Estimated Area (square metres)
Walls	2.5	0.6	8.00	307
Windows	5.5	-	-	77
Roof	2.5	0.3	2.50	408
Floor	2.6	0.6	8.00	408

The objective was to identify avoidable waste and to report recommendations for the actions considered most likely to produce a good return on outlay. Further investigation work necessary to supplement existing data would also be noted to allow for the better evaluation of potential savings.

Information to hand at the outset of the survey covered the building characteristics, as noted above, and limited data on the space heating/hot water loads and electricity consumption. This material is summarised below.

Space Heating and Hot Water

The space heating and hot water services for the site are provided from two boilerhouses which are marked on the plan. These serve the two quads and Annex A, and the mansion group of buildings respectively.

Both boilerhouses contain two gas oil-fired boilers one for space heating and one for hot water. No split was available of the oil consumption between the separate boilers or boilerhouses and the only information to hand was the schedule of total gas oil deliveries as compiled from the delivery dockets—see Table 9.3.

This information was, however, sufficient to make an approximate estimate of how the gas oil consumption was shared between space heating and hot water once it had been established that the heating was turned off at the beginning of June until the latter part of September. The cumulative graph of oil consumption month by month given in Figure 9.4 shows the summer, hot water only, load at around 4,000 litres per month. Assuming this load remains broadly constant throughout the year then some correlation might be expected between the derived space heating consumption data and degree days month by month. This exercise is undertaken in the table above the graph and shows an approximate relationship when allowance is made for the lower attendance levels over the Easter and Christmas periods etc.

Table 9.5 contains the basic details of the boilers together with the results of the consultant's combustion efficiency tests. Their operation is limited by flow temperature thermostats and time switches programmed to the periods also shown in Table 9.5.

Attention was drawn at the outset to whether the systems were suitable and it was suggested that the oil consumption for space heating purposes should be compared with a rule of thumb estimate of 0.75 therms per square foot a year, a figure considered broadly appropriate for this type and occupancy of building.

The efficiency of boiler operation would clearly be another factor for examination. Their condition, insulation, maintenance, time and temperature controls, suitability for size and type of load, facilities for monitoring boiler usage and oil consumption, and even the possibility of using other fuels or electricity would all have to be considered.

The efficiency of the distribution system, also, would need to be looked at including the time and temperature controls (their setting and operation), the insulation of the pipework and the position of the boiler plants in relation to their use points. Was there a case for discontinuing the boiler systems in favour of other types of heating?

TABLE 9.3: SUMMARY OF GAS OIL DELIVERIES

Delivery Date	Litres	Cost (£)
18/12/80	16,000	2,453
8/ 1/81	18,000	2,759
29/ 1/81	18,000	2,979
11/ 2/81	18,000	2,979
2/ 3/81	18,000	2,979
23/ 3/81	18,000	2,979
14/ 4/81	18,000	2,527
13/ 5/81	18,000	2,527
20/ 7/81	18,000	2,666
16/10/81	18,000	3,001
6/11/81	18,000	2,865
23/11/81	18,000	2,984
19/12/81	18,000	2,984
7/ 1/82	18,000	2,900
20/ 1/82	18,000	2,900
1/ 2/82	18,000	2,909

TABLE 9.5: BOILER SPECIFICATIONS AND EFFICIENCY TEST RESULTS

Average of several tests	Mansion		Quads	
	Space heating	Hot water	Space heating	Hot water
Make	Heatrae Aggressor	Robin Hood	Ideal Britannia	Robin Hood
Rating Btu/hour	2,000,000	500,000	2,152,000	532,000
Estimated age—years	14	15+	9	20+
Test CO_2 (%)	10.5	8.5	12.5	7.5
Test flue temperature $^{\circ}F$	680	760	545	1,005
Smoke Number	6	0	0	4
Flue loss (%)	23.2	30.2	17.9	43.0
Estimated other losses (%)	5.0	8.5	5.0	8.5
Overall boiler efficiency at MCR (%)	71.8	61.3	77.1	48.5

Note: Actual efficiencies will be five to ten per cent less than shown above, bearing in mind the frequently very low loads.

Boiler Operating Periods (time switches)

	On	Off—each day
Mansion Space Heating	04.30	23.00
Mansion Hot Water	04.30	22.30
Quads Space Heating	05.00	11.00
	+15.15	23.00
Quads Hot Water	04.00	10.00
	+14.00	22.00

Note: Manual override used to switch off when buildings are unoccupied—especially quads.

TABLE 9.4: GAS OIL CONSUMPTION BY MONTH
As deduced from the graph of cumulative deliveries above

Month	Consumption (litres)	Degree days	Net Consumption for Space Heating divided by degree days
J	36,000	340	94
F	31,000	369	73
M	28,000	243	99
A	20,000	245	65—Easter
My	15,000	147	75
Jn	4,000	81	-
Jy	4,000	39	-
A	4,000	41	-
S	5,000	69	-
O	22,000	227	79
N	30,000	246	106
D	29,000	494	51—Christmas

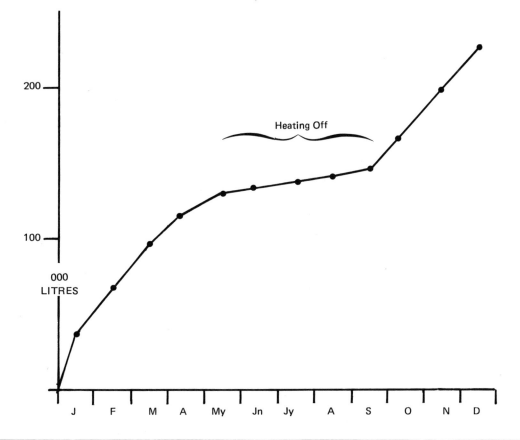

Electricity Consumption

A copy of a recent month's electricity bill appears in Table 9.6 and a monthly summary of the pertinent data for the past 12 months is given in Table 9.7.

The Electricity Board's demand meters are located in the electricity substation and sample readings are set out in Table 9.8. The small night-time electricity use, established by meter readings at midnight and 8.30 a.m., was found to be an average of 22 kilowatts.

Attention was drawn to whether the appropriate tariff had been selected and whether as much use was being made as possible of the cheaper off-peak facilities. The power factor would need to be checked to determine whether a case could be made for installing correction capacitors.

FIGURE 9.6: THE ELECTRICITY BILL

METER READINGS *		Consumption *	METER READINGS *		Consumption *
Present	Previous				
64192 UNITS X	61454 10.00	27380			

MAXIMUM DEMAND THIS MONTH	K.V.A. (Daytime) 88.0	K.V.A. (Night time)	ANNUAL MAXIMUM DEMAND	K.V.A. 96.0	Month Recorded JAN

DESCRIPTION OF CHARGE	No. OF UNITS OR K.V.A.	RATE	AMOUNT EXCLUSIVE OF TAX	VAT REG. No. 238 5679 21	
				Tax	% Rate
ANNUAL KVA 1	96.0	£6.650/12	53.20		00.00
MONTHLY KVA	88.0	£2.980	262.24		00.00
UNIT CHARGE	27380	2.892P	791.82		00.00
FUEL CLAUSE	27380	0.46200P	126.49		00.00
FIXED CHARGE	100		4.70		00.00
		TOTAL	1238.45	0.00	

NEXT NORMAL METER READING DATE:- 02 APR	M.D. THIS MONTH (KW) 86.0	COST OF FUEL PER TONNE 46.00	£ 1238.45 TOTAL DUE	15 MAR 1982 LATEST DATE FOR PAYMENT

* above 'E' = ESTIMATED. 'R' = METER REMOVED 'N' = NIGHT UNITS

TABLE 9.7: SUMMARY OF ELECTRICITY BILLS

	Days	kWh	Max kVA	kWh/day	Cost £
Jan 81	-	33,460	88	-	1,255
F	28	27,820	84	994	1,068
M	35	31,340	92	895	1,096
A	28	17,510	78	625	618
M	29	17,970	84	620	629
Ju	34	26,420	78	777	891
Jy	28	18,950	70	677	656
A	28	12,660	58	452	458
S	35	18,380	62	525	638
O	29	20,420	72	704	702
N	24	24,210	76	1,008	967
D	32	27,250	86	851	1,214
		276,390 kWh			£10,192 (average 3.7p)
Jan 82	38	40,960	96	1,078	1,735
F	25	27,380	88	1,095	1,238

TABLE 9.8: SAMPLE ELECTRICITY METER READINGS

Date	Time	Instantaneous kW load	Total kWh	Off Peak kWh	Maximum Demand kW	kVa
26.3.82	11.10	56	667,520	00,151	90	90
	12.33	-	667,582	00,151	90	90
	13.23	-	667,599	00,151	90	90
1.4.82	08.56	80	672,520	00,151	90	90
8.4.82	15.00	-	677,540	00,151	62*	66

*Meters had been reset since 1.4.82

The Consultant's Report

Reproduced below is the full text of the report on the college buildings prepared by David Yuill. It highlights two areas for immediate attention: bring into effect the cheap night rate option for which electricity meters were already installed and improve boiler combustion efficiency. Whilst costing very little, these measures result in annual savings of £1,700.00.

The Summary also recommends expenditure on insulation, which, in the case of the roof to the old quad, would bring a payback well within 18 months and in the case of Annex A within 2½ years. Important also are the recommendations to install time meters on the boilers and a temporary electric load recorder, available on loan from the Electricity Board, which would provide the data necessary for evaluating further measures.

The Main Report, which follows the Management Summary, is set out to the structure laid down by the Department of Energy for use by consultants employed in the Energy Survey Scheme. This type of approach and level of detail is to be expected by clients hiring a consultant under this scheme.

Management Summary

Energy Use

Consumption of energy in the twelve months to December 1981 was:-

	Cost £	Quantity	Energy equivalent Gigajoules (GJ)
Gas oil	36,000	228,000 litre	8,679
Electricity	10,192	276,390 kWh	995

Other energy consumption, outside the scope of this survey, included electricity for pumping water and LPG for cooking and supplementary space heating.

Summary of Recommendations

Recommendation	Estimated Annual Savings		Estimated Cost of Implementation
	£	%	£
1.1 Install time meters on four boilers			60
1.2 Install temporary electric load recorder			100
1.3 Use cheap night rate facility on existing electricity tariff	980		
1.4 Increased attention at servicing to combustion efficiency of boilers, especially mansion space heating boiler	720	2	–
1.5 Insulate loft of old quad building	1,340		1,760
1.6 Replace quads hot water boiler with off-peak electric heating	*		500
1.7 Insulate roof, walls and floor of Annex A, if kept	3,600 (full use)		9,000
1.8 Decentralise mansion hot water system	*		4,000
1.9 Consider more thermostatic radiator valves and sectional heating controls only after evidence from boiler metering	*		

* signifies saving to be indicated by proposed boiler metering.

Further Investigation Recommended

2.1 Use information from electric load recording to highlight avoidable waste and demand charges.

2.2 Analyse individual boiler fuel consumptions to assess more accurately potential savings noted in the report and identify further possible economies.

Energy Management

Institute weekly monitoring of oil and electricity consumption as basis for progressive energy conservation.

Main Report

Boilers

Specifications and average combustion efficiency test results on the four boilers in use were as follows. (See Table 9.5). All boilers are of sectional construction.

Service contract arrangements have recently been changed. It is considered essential that such attention is given twice a year, and that CO_2 and temperature checks are made at servicing in future.

Mansion space heating boiler—suitably sized for its duty. Service engineers report difficulty in achieving efficient combustion with reasonably low smoke numbers. The furnace operates above atmospheric pressure and fumes (smell of SO_2) escape through defective joints. Some sooting of the heat transfer surfaces was evident, and contributes to the rather high stack temperature. Two cracked sections were recently replaced, and the boiler may well need replacement before long. Meanwhile a high standard of attention should be given to maintaining the best possible combustion conditions on this, the most hard working of all the boilers.

Unless excavation were practical, there is too little headroom in this boilerhouse to transfer the otherwise suitable Britannia boiler from the quads boilerhouse, presently very underloaded.

Mansion hot water boiler—not capable of high efficiency, but some improvement of combustion should be possible by reduction of excess air.

In the light of future metered oil consumption, consider decentralising the mansion hot water service, with new main supply in kitchen area and three or four other separate electrically heated (off-peak) in toilet and bathroom areas of the old building. Heat losses from the present extensive pumped circuits are considerable.

Quads space heating boiler—is potentially efficient but several times too big for present duty (due to demolition of former annexes), and would be even more so should the Annex A load be removed.

Quads hot water boiler—very old, with improvised conversion to oil firing, not capable of efficient working. Would be redundant if off-peak electric water heating were installed (see later).

No split of oil consumption is available between the four boilers, or even between the total space heating and total hot water load. Installation of elapsed time meters (cost about £15 each) on each is recommended which, in conjunction with weekly total oil monitoring, will permit accurate evaluation of potential savings in these areas. For immediate purposes, an estimate of 80 per cent space and 20 per cent hot water is taken.

Space Heating

Estimated annual oil cost £29,000. Overall therms per square foot per annum for total floor area seems quite moderate at 0.84, but partly so because of reduced heating according to occupancy in the quads and annex, making firm estimates of load even more difficult. This oil cost may possibly be reduced by as much as 15 per cent by attention to boiler efficiency, heating control and building insulation.

Recent improvement of weather compensation, existing boiler and pump time and temperature controls and vigilance by domestic staff have produced a reasonable level of heating control with the possible exception of the old quad, Annex A and some offices in the mansion. Possible further refinements such as additional thermostatic radiator valves in those areas and even more sophisticated sectional heating control should be assessed later, with the benefit of several months' additional heating oil monitoring.

Most visible heating mains were adequately lagged, except some in the mansion attic, which should be attended to.

Building Insulation

Annex A is outstandingly bad, lacking adequate insulation to roof, walls and exposed floor. The heat loss is 3.6 times what it would be if insulated to present new domestic standards, and if operated 14 hours per day through the heating season would cost £5,000 per annum in fuel. If retained in use, this building would certainly justify thorough insulation (subject to structural soundness). A critical review of its future is urged.

Loft insulation (100 mm thick) of the old quad is recommended. This would cost about £1,700, reducing fuel requirement by £1,340 per annum.

Although insulation standards of remaining buildings are only moderate, no other major instances for economic improvement were noted. The extensive floor to ceiling windows of the concourse have already been double glazed.

Ventilation Control

Generally quite good, with door closing springs, draught excluding lobbies where necessary.

Hot Water Systems

Until availability of metered consumption, roughly estimated at 20 per cent of total oil, costing £7,000 per annum.

Mansion hot water boiler is below 60 per cent actual efficiency. There is extensive pumped distribution to widely separate small consumers and the boiler/storage calorifier are well away from the main use area. Subject to confirmation by boiler metering, recommend replacement of boiler and system by:-

   —new boiler or off-peak electric hot water storage in kitchen/laundry/D block area

   —small self contained electric hot water systems at three or four points in the mansion old building serving toilets and bathrooms. Off-peak heating where appropriate.

Old quad/Annex A oil costs are at least as great as day rate electricity.

	Cost per useful therm
Present oil heating	114 p
Day rate electric, 3.7p per kWh average	108 p
Off-peak electric	47.5p

A change to off-peak electric heating is recommended, using existing 1,000 gallon storage or, if Annex A closes, a new storage tank within old quad building.

Electricity

The EMEB Tariff DMA is appropriate, but advantage is not taken of the cheap night rate facility. Off-peak meter installed, so no cost involved. One overnight check indicated saving of £980 per annum. This can be rechecked, particularly by reference to proposed load recording.
   Power factor at maximum demand is near unity; no case for power factor correction.
   Although considerable waste occurred in the past from unnecessary lights left on, this is now largely reduced by time switches in offices, concourse, squash courts, etc.
   Much tungsten lighting remains inside buildings, and its progressive replacement by more efficient luminaires is recommended, although quick returns will be hard to find. The concourse is one area for which such proposals could be invited.
   There is very little electric space heating.
   Temporary installation of an electric load recorder is recommended, from which it will be possible to assess the potential for saving by:-

   —use of off-peak power
   —reduction of maximum demand charges
   —further avoidance of waste.

Monitoring

Although many common sense measures have been practised, and effective controls installed, little or no evidence has been collected of the effect such practices have on fuel and power consumption and costs. Simple weekly monitoring of consumption is recommended, from which the effect of changing conditions on energy consumption can be observed. In this way the most beneficial methods can be identified and, where possible, adopted as standard. Monitoring thereby provides a basis for consolidating improvements in practice and for progressive saving over the years. Suggested weekly readings are:-

—electricity: kWh consumption, total and off-peak, latest kVA maximum demand level.

—oil: elapsed time meters on each boiler (converted to oil consumption by appropriate factor). Storage tank contents gauges (plus deliveries) to confirm boiler meter totals.

APPENDIX I:
SPEAKERS, WRITERS AND CONTRIBUTORS TO
THE ENERGY MANAGERS' WORKSHOPS

Course Director

G A D Coghlan
10 Hamilton Avenue
Birmingham B17

The Role of the Energy Manager

T Henshaw
Group Electrical Engineer
Amey Roadstone Corporation Ltd
Group Operational Services Centre
The Ridge, Chipping Sodbury
Bristol BS17 6AY
Tel: (0454) 316000

B Lubert
Chief Engineer
Marks & Spencer plc
Michael House
Baker Street
London W1

P Ibbotson
Company Engineer
J Sainsbury plc
Stamford House
London SE1 9LL

R Harrison
Energy Conservation Executive
British Home Stores
Marylebone House
129 Marylebone Road
London NW1

Energy Survey

D M Yuill
Industrial Energy Consultant
5 Blakebrook
Kidderminster
Worcs DY11 6AP
Tel: (0562) 4822

Lighting

Lighting Industry Federation
Swan House
207 Balham High Road
London SW17 7BQ
Tel: 01-675 5432

V G Neal
Manager, Energy Advisory Group
Philips Lighting Ltd
PO Box 298
City House, 420-430 London Road
Croydon CR9 3QR
Tel: 01-689 2166

M Wells and D L Spencer (London)
Thorn EMI Lighting plc
Thorn House
Aston Church Road
Saltley Trading Estate
Birmingham B8 1BE
Tel: 021-327 1535

Boiler and Furnace Efficiency

C W E Hardy
Green Lane House
Fordingbridge
Hants SP6 1HT
Tel: (0425) 52093

Building Services

K Spiers
Manager, Energy Department
John Laing Research & Development Ltd
Manor Way
Borehamwood
Herts
Tel: 01-953 6144

Insulation

Eurisol-UK
St Paul's House
Edison Road
Bromley
Kent BR2 0EP
Tel: 01-466 6719

A J Williams
Marketing Director
Kitson Insulation Contractors Ltd
Latchford House
40-50 Riverdene Road
Ilford
Essex IG1 2DS
Tel: 01-514 3100

M Wright
Technical Product Manager
Gyproc Ltd
Whitehouse Industrial Estate
Runcorn
Cheshire
Tel: (0928) 712627

Controls

Hevac
Unit 3
Phoenix House
Phoenix Way
Heston
Middlesex TW5 9ND
Tel: 01-897 2848/9

F Ranson
Product Manager, Energy Systems
Johnson Control Systems Ltd
PO Box 79
Stone Hill Green
Westley Down
Swindon
Wilts SN5 7DD
Tel: (0793) 26141

P Lovering
Sauter Automation
Sussex House
Park Lane
Crowborough
East Sussex
Tel: (089 26) 64244

Finance

B Healey
Consultant
Watendlath
62 Putnoe Heights
Bedford MK41 8EB
Tel: (0234) 52966

Transport

W Kirkland
Controller of Engineering, Property Services
South Yorkshire PTE
1 Exchange Street
Sheffield
S2 5SZ

Gas *

R Jones
Co-ordinator, Conservation Projects
Marketing Division
British Gas Corporation
Rivermill House
152 Grosvenor Road
London SW1V 3JL

Electricity *

E J Bell
Energy Technologist
Marketing Department
Electricity Council
30 Millbank
London SW1

B Booth
Head of Planning & Industrial Marketing
Electricity Council
30 Millbank
London SW1

Coal *

A Williams
Chief Maintenance, Energy Engineer
National Coal Board
The Lodge
South Parade
Doncaster DN1 2DX

Oil *

A D C Turner
Chairman
UK PIA
Texaco Ltd
1 Knightsbridge Green
London SW1

M Ward
Total Oil
Rodgelands
Bank Lane
Abberley
Worcester WR6 6BQ

denotes Management Board Representative

APPENDIX II:

REGIONAL ENERGY CONSERVATION OFFICES

Northern Region

Stanegate House
Groat Market
Newcastle upon Tyne
NE1 1YN
Tel: (0632) 324722, Ext 218
Telex: 5317

North Western Region

Sunley Building
Piccadilly Plaza
Manchester M1 4BA
Tel: 061-236 2171, Ext 640
Telex: 667104

Yorkshire and Humberside Region

Priestley House
Park Row
Leeds LS1 5LF
Tel: (0532) 443171, Ext 353
Telex: 557925

West Midlands Region

Ladywood House
Stephenson Street
Birmingham B2 4DT
Tel: 021-632 4111, Ext 539
Telex: 337021

Scotland (Scottish Office)

Scottish Economic Planning Department
Energy Division
Room 6/54
New St Andrews House
St James Centre
Edinburgh EH1 3SX
Tel: 031-556 8400
Telex: 727301

Northern Ireland

Department of Economic Development
21 Linenhall Street
Belfast 2
Tel: (0232) 230555
(Temporary address)

East Midlands Region

Severns House
20 Middle Pavement
Nottingham NG1 7DW
Tel: (0602) 56181, Ext 285-4-3
Telex: 37143

South Eastern Region

(i) Southern Area

Room 583
Charles House
375 Kensington High Street
London W14 8QH
Tel: 01-603 2060, Ext 245
Telex: 25991

(ii) Eastern Area

Room 582
Charles House
375 Kensington High Street
London W14 8QH
Tel: 01-603 2060, Ext 248
Telex: 25991

South Western Region

The Pithay
Bristol BS1 2PB
Tel: (0272) 291071, Ext 205
Telex: 44214

Wales (Welsh Office)

Industry Department
Cathays Park
Cardiff CF1 3NQ
Tel: (0222) 823545
Telex: 498228